# RELENTLESS

How to Become Unstoppable in the Midst of Tremendous Opposition, Immense Adversity, and Daunting Resistance

By

Rebecca Bell, Gloria De Guzman, Miriam De Leon, M.D.,
Leni Hufana-Del Prado, Ferdinand R. Gaite,
Maria Josephine Trono-Lumawig, Jackie Lansangan-Morey,
Billy A. San Juan, Rev. Dante Eleazar Simon,
Paulyn Jean Rosell Ubial, M.D., M.P.H.

# RELENTLESS

How to Become Unstoppable in the Midst
of Tremendous Opposition, Immense
Adversity, and Daunting Resistance

By

Rebecca Bell, Gloria De Guzman, Miriam De Leon, M.D.,
Leni Hufana-Del Prado, Ferdinand R. Gaite,
Maria Josephine Trono-Lumawig, Jackie Lansangan-Morey,
Billy A. San Juan, Rev. Dante Eleazar Simon,
Paulyn Jean Rosell Ubial, M.D., M.P.H.

A Collaborative Work by Graduates of the
University of the Philippines Integrated School,
Class of 1979 and Members of their Families

Copyright © 2020 by Customer Strategy Academy and © 2020 Jackie Morey

**ALL RIGHTS RESERVED.** This book contains material protected under International and Federal Laws and Treaties. Any unauthorized reprint or use of this material is prohibited. No portion of this book may be used, reproduced, stored in a retrieval system, or transmitted in any form or by any means — electronic, mechanical, photocopy, recording, scanning, or other — without express written permission from the authors or publisher, except for a brief quotation in critical reviews or articles. It is illegal to copy this book, post it to a website, or distribute it by any other means without permission from the authors and publisher.

**Published by**

Customer Strategy Academy, LLC
16212 Bothell Everett Hwy, Suite F , Mill Creek, WA 98012
Publisher Jackie Morey's email: CustomerStrategyAcademy@gmail.com

**Copyright Use and Public Information**

Unless otherwise noted, images have been used according to public information laws.

ISBN: 978-1-7332501-3-9 Paperback

**Limits of Liability and Disclaimer of Warranty**

The authors and publisher shall not be liable for the reader's misuse of this material. This book is for strictly informational and educational purposes.

Scripture quotations taken from the New American Standard Bible® (NASB), Copyright © 1960, 1962, 1963, 1968, 1971, 1972, 1973, 1975, 1977, 1995 by The Lockman Foundation Used by permission. www.Lockman.org. The Holy Bible, English Standard Version® (ESV®) Copyright © 2001 by Crossway, a publishing ministry of Good News Publishers. All rights reserved. Scriptures marked NLT are taken from the HOLY BIBLE, NEW LIVING TRANSLATION (NLT): Scriptures taken from the HOLY BIBLE, NEW LIVING TRANSLATION, Copyright© 1996, 2004, 2007 by Tyndale House Foundation. Used by permission of Tyndale House Publishers, Inc., Carol Stream, Illinois 60188. All rights reserved. Used by permission. Scriptures marked NKJV are taken from the NEW KING JAMES VERSION (NKJV): Scripture taken from the NEW KING JAMES VERSION®. Copyright© 1982 by Thomas Nelson, Inc. Used by permission. All rights reserved. Scriptures marked NIV are taken from the NEW INTERNATIONAL VERSION (NIV): Scripture taken from THE HOLY BIBLE, NEW INTERNATIONAL VERSION ®. Copyright© 1973, 1978, 1984, 2011 by Biblica, Inc.™. Used by permission of Zondervan.

**Disclaimer**

The views expressed are those of the authors and do not reflect the official policy or position of the publisher or Customer Strategy Academy. This publication is designed to provide accurate and authoritative information regarding the subject matter covered. It is sold with the understanding that the publisher is not engaged in rendering legal, accounting, clinical or other professional advice. If legal advice or other expert assistance is required, the services of a competent professional should be sought. The opinions expressed by the authors in this book are not endorsed by Customer Strategy Academy, and are the sole responsibility of the author rendering the opinion.

# DEDICATION AND ACKNOWLEDGEMENTS

**Rebecca Bell** – I dedicate this piece to my hero, my Mother. And I would like to express my gratitude for my dear friend, Aly Vildosola, who has been a bottomless source of encouragement during my writing journey.

**Gloria De Guzman** – I would like to dedicate this chapter to my mother, brother and sister – they are my anchor and the colors of my rainbow, to all VSO staff and fellow volunteers – for their immeasurable efforts to help create a brighter world, to the Catholic priests and sisters whose lives and work intersected with mine – for giving me a glimpse of the depth of their love for the vulnerable people of Karamoja and their enviable commitment to their mission, and lastly to my father, who passed on many years ago, for modeling hard work, compassion and relentlessness.

I would like to thank Amifaith Fider-Reyes and Jackie Morey for their generosity, trust and patience, Jackie and her team for their editing, and UPIS batchmates for the inspiration. I am deeply grateful to Teresita Vivas Guillen for constantly reminding me that my life has been made richer by my volunteering journey and that I need to share my story with the world; to Neil Mark Hubiera for giving me a journal that spurred me to muse about my experiences and document them; to Maloy Quesada Tiongson, Catherine Calamiong, Michael Saludaga, Celina Fong, Ching Abril, Meerna Dabalus and Rebecca Pino for opening doors and windows to places and opportunities I did not know of, to the Surbaybors and dear friends from DEAL, ERC, OVCSSS and OASIS for the encouragement and prayers, and to Sr. Margie, Sr. Paulina and Sr. Maria Eugenia, RSCJ, and Fr. Jimmy for truly embodying relentlessness, selflessness and missionary work.

**Miriam De Leon, M.D.** – I dedicate this book to all those who face adversity in any form and to the extraordinary people who journey alongside them. And, to my family: Frank, Rebecca, Nathan and Daniel. You have all moved me to become more than I could ever imagine.

**Leni Hufana-Del Prado** – I dedicate this book to God, Who has given me purpose and guidance, to my family, my husband Patrick, Timothy, Silas and his lovely wife Nikki , whom I love and has been my inspiration. I acknowledge the following persons who have inspired and given me permission to peep into their lives, probe and write their riveting life stories. I acknowledge the people who have given me their eye witness accounts of the journey of their loved one or contributed to the completion of the stories: Pastor Shane Wildermoth, Bianca Rodriguez-Gallego and Pastor Albit Rodriguez, Michael and Sandy Uysiuseng, Ging, Marie, and Dr. Candy Tanchi-Pedro for the lyrics of her beautiful composition.

**Ferdinand Gaite** – I dedicate this book to my family, friends, comrades and the supreme being who have all helped mold me to what I have achieved now, my parents – may they rest in peace – who provided for my physical, mental and general well-being, my family whose support remains steadfast, my friends and comrades who continue to be with us in the struggle, and the Lord Almighty for the great plan in store for us.

**Maria Josephine Trono-Lumawig** – I wrote this book chapter to honor God who never failed to be my guide, the Sun to whom I look up to, through life even at times when I dismiss His nudge. His faithfulness relentlessly brought me to what I am doing now – teaching. My husband, Francis, has always been a big support in everything I do, including during the late nights of writing this chapter.

My children remain my inspirations and the major reasons why I get up early in the morning. I offer this book chapter to my parents, Jun and Letty Trono, who are both teachers and from whom I got the 'genes' to teach. While I shied away from the idea of being a teacher as I walked through my career in the garment industry, the Lord used those genes as a strong force to finally lead me to being a Professor in the University. To my students, present and past, many of whom are having babies now, it is and will always be my pleasure to serve you. Thank you! This chapter book is for all of you, my loves.

**Jackie Lansangan-Morey** – I dedicate this book to the relentless Ekklesia Women-Warrior friends who are indeed relentless in faith, relentless in hope, and relentless in love. I also dedicate this book to my Husband Jim, our children Michael and Alyssa, to all my extended family members here in the U.S., Canada, and the Philippines, as well as to all my friends near and far.

I'd like to acknowledge and give all the glory to Abba Yahweh, Yeshua Ha Maschiach, and Ruach Hakodesh – Who continue lavishing their love, wisdom, revelation, and insight upon me, and Who continue to train and empower me to be relentless in my *faith*, relentless in *hope* and relentless in *love*.

**Billy A. San Juan** – I dedicate this book to my mother Betty – who is still going strong at 87. I'd like to thank my wife Marian – who has patiently withstood my moods and has always been at my side to support me, my sweet daughter Pacey – who is my constant source of joy, many thanks to Sam – my spiritual brother, and mentor, and to LPL – my model of a genuine leader.

**Rev. Dante Eleazar Simon** – I dedicate this book to my wife, Vivelyn Pascual, who is relentless in so many ways. I also dedicate this book to my three sons – David, Stephen and Dante Jr. To God be the glory!

**Paulyn Jean Rosell Ubial, M.D., M.P.H.** – I would like to dedicate this book to my parents who are now in a better place, who molded me and my six sibling into who we are today and inculcated the values of industry, integrity, patience, compassion and patriotism in us, Prof. Neon Corro Rosell from Daanbantayan, Cebu and Ms. Maria Doronilla Buenaflor from Dumangas, Iloilo and Mlang, North Cotabato.

I would also like to acknowledge the people who encouraged me and kept faith in me throughout my public health journey: my immediate family – my husband Edwin and only son Karl, who moved with me whenever I got re-assigned anywhere in the Philippines. And of course, my colleagues in the DOH where I spent 29 years of my journey, my classmates in Medicine and UPIS who believed in my advocacy on anti-corruption and helping the less fortunate and who were always ready to support and assist me.

# TABLE OF CONTENTS

Foreword ........................................................................................1

Chapter 1: Full Circle ..................................................................5

Chapter 2: When the Wind Blows: Return to Africa ...........21

Chapter 3: Sunshine Boy ..........................................................53

Chapter 4: Not Without Tears..................................................67

Chapter 5: The Journey Thus Far .......................................... 137

Chapter 6: The Sunflowers Grow Even After Summer.... 147

Chapter 7: Relentless in Faith, Relentless in Hope, Relentless in Love.................................................. 173

Chapter 8: Further Down the Road ...................................... 199

Chapter 9: The Character of Relentless Leaders................ 225

Chapter 10: Relentless Quest................................................... 253

# FOREWORD

From the perspective that each writer had some connection with the University of the Philippines Integrated School Class of 1979, this would be the second collaborative book.

The first collaborative book was called UNSTOPPABLE. It was about the story of 14 members of the aforementioned high school class, and a look back at how far they, we, had each gone.

UNSTOPPABLE was an easy book to write. We were writing from our hearts.

We wrote about those we loved, those we lived for, and those we laughed with. From what everyone had written, it might as well have been called a book on GRATITUDE.

We were so happy with that book, and, even happier that it made so many more people happier.

Now this book RELENTLESS, is the story of Rebecca, Gloria, Leni, Josephine, Billy, Ferdinand, Miriam, Jackie, Eleazar and Paulyn. They are relentless.

They are relentless in their faith. In a world filled with overwhelming materialism, these people believe and hope in a purpose, and in something or someone larger than their very beings. To that larger Being, these people have subsumed their very existence.

This is what Leni, Jackie, Josephine, and Eleazar have written about. As Josephine would say, everything works for the good of those who love God. To be relentless, means, to believe.

They are relentless about family. None of them ever said, that, their family was perfect. But, they all traced a profound sense of security and identity to it, that, each time Rebecca would touch her palm to her cheek, there was the kiss that would always make her feel, that, "Mommy loves me." There is always something unconditional in the way we relate to anyone in our family. To be relentless, means, to love.

They are relentless about giving. Like the wind, after which her new friends had named her, Gloria saw that there was no measure to the generosity of the human spirit to empathize, to search for solidarity and to serve. There is no limit, not even the sky, to what a mother would do to see her son happy. This mother is Miriam. There is no limit to the will to serve the people, even if one was deprived of the wherewithal of a government position to pursue this goal, like Paulyn. To be relentless, means, to sacrifice.

They are relentless in the pursuit of their dreams. Despite the limitations offered by their personal circumstances, or the people around them like their family or colleagues, these people saw a better reality for themselves and for others. Even if the situation seemed surreal, as Ferdinand would say, some things cannot co-exist with democracy and the sanctity of life. Because even if one had to heed a father's advice, to look out for one's safety always, that same father never asked Billy to stop doing the things he believed in. To be relentless, means, to always forge on.

Read more about being relentless from Rebecca, Gloria, Leni, Josephine, Billy, Ferdinand, Miriam, Jackie, Eleazar and Paulyn. See how they live their seemingly ordinary lives. They are like us, facing day to day battles. They deal with the reality of family life. They endure professional challenges. They experience trials and tests of faith. They suffer the same consequences from a natural calamity such as a typhoon. And they are each also doing their best to live the new normal with circumstances that began in 2020.

More importantly, see how they are doing it. And see how you too, can be relentless.

## *Judge Maria Amifaith S. Fider-Reyes*

Presiding Judge of the Regional Trial Court (RTC)-Third Judicial Region, Branch 42, City of San Fernando Pampanga

Acting Judge of the RTC-National Capital Judicial Region (NCJR) in Branch 51 Manila, Branch 147 and Branch 61 in Makati City, and Branch 99 in Quezon City

#1 International Bestselling Author

# CHAPTER 1

# Full Circle

By Rebecca Bell

**Secret Mother-Daughter Power**

My mother's hands are trained to heal. They are the hands of a physician. They can adjust necks and lift limbs, restoring movements in places made stiff by injury or time. She keeps her nails short and polish-free, but her hands are anything but plain.

Her grip is unusually strong. I remember struggling to hold my head still as she brushed out my hair after a bath. But those same hands can make delicate sculptures out of paper and bring birds to life with watercolors. They are the hands of an artist and a nurturer.

They fidget when she is upset or anxious, tidying and straightening anything within her reach. But they can also apply lipstick and eyeliner in a moving vehicle with lightning speed and laser-point precision. My mother's hands are tender but strong, beautiful in their complexity.

Starting kindergarten sounded exciting until I found out that it meant having to leave home. What a cruel trick. My school was only blocks away. If you took a left past the smelly gingko tree and another left at the tall ivy wall, it was the building on the right after the stop light.

It might as well have been on the moon.

The questions banged around my head like bumper cars. Would my parents forget about me if I left home? What if I wanted to tell them I love them? Why couldn't they come to school with me? Could I go to work with them? If only adults could go to work, couldn't I become an adult instead of a kindergartener? I felt like a salmon being pushed from the river too soon.

One night, Mom added Audrey Penn's "The Kissing Hand" to our bedtime book queue. The story was about a baby racoon named Chester and his mother, Mrs. Racoon. Chester experienced the same dread about leaving home for school. I felt understood. Mrs. Racoon helped Chester overcome his fear by teaching him the secret of "The Kissing Hand". She took Chester's baby paw in hers and kissed the middle of his palm and said, *"Now whenever you feel lonely and need a little loving from home,"* Mrs. Racoon said, "just press your hand to your cheek and think, *'Mommy loves you. Mommy loves you.'* And that very kiss will jump to your face and fill you with toasty warm thoughts."

When we got to this part of the book, Mom scooped my tiny hand in hers – those hands I love so much – and gently unfurled my fingers like flower petals. She planted a kiss right in the middle of my open palm. My own supply of Mommy love. Relief washed over me, instantly. I suspected that she wasn't as scared about leaving home as I was, but I kissed her palm anyway, just in case.

Reading "The Kissing Hand" became an integral part of my bedtime routine, along with brushing teeth and preparing my uniform. The palm kisses were our secret mother-daughter power.

The ritual of "The Kissing Hand" was one of my earliest memories of abstracting the idea of love. It was a lesson in harnessing the power of tenderness to give me the courage to face the unknown. *"And what does the kiss mean, Boopsie?"*, Mom would ask me each night, after adorning my palm with a fresh kiss. *"Mommy loves me,"* I would answer, empowered with my fresh kiss. *"Mommy loves me."*

## The Journey from Surgery to Recovery

Nothing could prepare me for the sight of my mother lying on a hospital bed after back surgery. On the day of her procedure, my husband – Jason and I had just gotten off a flight and came straight to the hospital from the airport. My father had called while we were in the taxi to let us know that mom had made it through the surgery.

We entered her hospital room, packs still slung over our backs. My breath caught in my throat at the sight of her listless body. When Papa said she was stable, I just assumed she would be awake when we got there. I had not considered that she needed time to regain consciousness and would still be groggy. I was *deeply* unsettled by her stillness.

My mother is not an idle person. For as long as I can remember, she had been the first one in the family to wake up. She rose with the sun and stayed in motion until long after dark, resting only after she had made sure that everyone's affairs were in order. But *that* day in the hospital, she lay eerily still.

I was eager to see her in action, again. Eager to see her do normal "Mom" things, like scribbling a note on a post-it, flipping through her day planner, or looking something up on her phone through her red reading glasses. I wanted to hear narrate her cooking in her talk show host voice or listen to her run through vocal warmups and drills while making tea. If only she would open her eyes…

Jason once told me that the heart is an amazing muscle because it never rests. From the moment it is formed until the day it dies, the heart tirelessly pumps blood to the rest of the body, giving it life. In this sense, Mom is *the heart of our family* – ceaseless, steady, essential. But there she lay in front of me, motionless and fragile. My eyes could hardly make sense of it.

I wanted her out of that hospital room, away from insidious beeping machines. Away from the harsh fluorescent lights as blindingly white as the scratchy starched sheets; away from the sterile scents that stung my eyes and throat.

The questions buzzed inside my head, giving me a headache. Was the surgery successful? How long would she be in pain? How long does it take for bones to regrow? Was there still threat of paralysis? I wanted answers. I wanted to talk to her.

When she did eventually open her eyes, I was able to breathe properly again. I was relieved for her, but also for the rest of us. I sat by her hospital bed and took her hand in mine, as gently as she held mine when I was a child.

During her week in the hospital, we became her shadows, desperately trying to comfort her or entertain her in any way we could. Fetching water, adjusting pillows. It must have been strange for her to be tended to, I thought, when she's been the one who tended to everyone else.

One night, I was watching her get ready for bed. After she finished brushing her teeth, she touched my arm and said, *"I would like to brush my hair."* She pointed to the wooden closet in the corner, where her bag was. I fetched the black travel-sized hairbrush and brought it to her like a puppy with a bone. I offered to brush it for her so she would not have to strain her back by reaching above her head. She hesitated for a moment before accepting my offer.

Her hair is thick and black like my middle brother's, Nathan. She had it cut short just before the surgery so it would be less of a hassle. Even for her own surgery, she was prepared.

When I tightened my grip on the handle, it made me think of how my head would move when mom would brush my hair as a kid. It made me nervous. In that moment, I realized that as nervous as I was, *she* was the one who had just faced her own mortality. She was the one who had been cut open and stitched back together.

I smoothed down the brushed hair with my other hand after every stroke to get rid of static. *"How's that, Ma?"* I asked when I was done brushing. She ran her fingers through her hair and nodded in approval. Then she whispered, *"Thank you"* in a voice so soft it cracked my heart.

How do you comfort the person who comforts you? How do you restore a mother's strength when it's been taken from her? I picked the fallen hairs off of her shoulder, and kissed her cheek before she dozed off to sleep.

The day she was discharged from the hospital was a happy day for *everyone*, especially our dear labradoodle, Mindy. The house felt right with her in it, again. And now she could convalesce in the comfort of her own home.

The recovery instructions from her surgeon were straightforward. There was a list of meds for managing pain and maintaining blood pressure. She needed lots of rest with periodic short walks. Her incision had to be washed gently and covered with gauze and special tape. I found comfort in the clarity of healing a physical wound.

But not all of her wounds were physical. She had to adapt

to the disruption to her career She had to endure us, her nagging family, constantly reminding her to mind her movements. *"Mom, no twisting,"* as she reached for something behind her. *"Mom, no bending,"* as she tried to pick something off the floor. My fear of her hurting herself before recovery conflicted with my own discomfort of being yet *another* person telling her what she could and could not do.

One night, we were in the kitchen having dinner, just the two of us. She was quieter than usual that evening. Her incision was stinging, and the pain medicine hadn't kicked in yet. I would have normally tried to ask her questions, but my gut told me that it wasn't the right time to engage her. I decided to try something different.

We had seen "My Fair Lady" at Lincoln Center earlier that year before her surgery. To cut the silence, I played the soundtrack for background noise. Upon hearing the intro chords to the song, "Wouldn't It Be Loverly," she stood up from the kitchen table. She walked to the adjacent room, to get closer to the speaker. I had the feeling she did not want to be followed, so I stayed seated. She belted the song at the top of her lungs, from start to finish, filling the whole house with her heart-rending song. The surgery had forced her to give up huge parts of herself: her independence, her privacy…and her peace. I wish the surgeon had left detailed instructions about how to deal with *that* type of loss.

Over the next few weeks, we made new memories together as a family. We listened to the songs of "Wicked" in the car.

We did crossword puzzles in the waiting room before her check-up. She helped me practice my Tagalog every morning in the kitchen while overseeing my attempts at cooking breakfast. Even dining out and going to movies became possible, as long as we remembered her blue seat cushion. It was remarkable to see how many people checked in on her. Every day, we received sweet messages of loved ones: our dear friends from neighborhood, her fellow choir members, friends, and family abroad. Each text and email was a message of tenderness to help see her through recovery.

After a month at home, you could hardly tell she had major back surgery. She still could not lift or twist the way she used to, but there was a renewed spring in her step. By that time, it was time for me to leave New York to move into our apartment in San Francisco.

It was one of the *hardest* goodbyes in my life.

She had my brother, my cousin, and my father in the house. She assured me she would be fine. The day I left, I looked back at the house. I felt like a little kid again, terrified to leave home.

A few months later, I got a call. Mom's 40th high school reunion was happening at the end of the year and she was trying to decide if she would go. We were all excited at the prospect of Mom attending. The family agreed that a celebration would be good for her spirits.

The *problem* was that the reunion was to take place in the Philippines, *nine thousand miles* away from home. The question flashed in my mind: had she recovered enough? She was strong enough to walk on her own but traveling internationally was a whole other ball game! It involved hours of sitting and carrying bags. She could go, but she would need a chaperone.

*This* is how I ended up crashing the UPIS Class of 1979's 40th reunion.

Six months after her surgery, Mom and I found ourselves in the Philippines on a bus with thirty of her giddy batchmates, inching its way up the western coastline of Luzon, headed for Ilocos Norte. The further north we went, the further away we got from the smog that chokes Metro Manila daily.

When we finally arrived, we poured out of the bus and stretched our legs. I retrieved our suitcases from the underbelly of the bus and followed the crowd through the wooden entrance gate between two tall bushes.

A cobblestone path stretched out in front of us, lined with fountains and lush green plants. The soft moss had grown through the cracks of the path. Nature reclaiming her land. But the stones had shifted and made the path uneven. Mom was wrapped up in a conversation and I waited for her to walk in front of me so I could have a clear view of her steps. She had been walking fine since we left New York. I *certainly* did not want to embarrass her by reminding her to be careful *every* five seconds, so I kept a respectful distance behind her. But I was prepared to drop everything and lunge if I saw so much as a wobble.

We had arrived just in time to see the local fishermen pull in the catch. The beach, one uninterrupted stripe of beige. The sand, another hazardous surface to survive. I placed Mom's hand on my arm as we walked. The hair-thin horizon traced endless blue, barely separating sea from sky.

The sea winds drowned out the collective chatter as we watched a few dozen locals slowly drag in a fishing net the size of a soccer field. There were some toddlers crouched in the shallow waters yanking tiny anchovies from beneath the net. One kid banged the net with his fist and a sprinkle of anchovies burst in the air like silver confetti, glimmering in the late-afternoon sun.

The beach dogs caught Mom's attention. There is no one in my life who loves dogs as much as she does. She smiled, watching the dogs pace back and forth, patiently waiting to pick at leftovers. The rim of her big, black sun hat flapped in the wind. It felt like we were standing at the edge of the world. The hospital room seemed like a lifetime ago.

Back at the resort, Tita Beth had organized a game of charades. The theme: guess the Ilocano word. They played the game mostly in Tagalog, speaking so quickly that I didn't bother to ask for translations. But I didn't mind. In fact, I preferred to hear them speak at their natural pace. I didn't have to know exactly what they were saying. I recognized the bubbly sounds of inside jokes and the squeals of rediscovered memories.

I had forgotten the last time I saw my mom laugh *that* hard. I fought back tears. It was powerful to watch her be embraced by her peers, some of whom she kept up with in New York. Others she had not seen in years. But time and distance had not weakened their bond at all. Even though they lived oceans apart, their commitment to stay in touch had preserved the tenderness between them. The warmth in their collective bond was unique and infectious. Not only were they determined to have a good time with each other, they were also eager to spread the joy. And anytime I had a confused look on my face, someone would leap to answer any question I had. They cherished me because they cherished my mother.

A plate appeared in front of me carrying a long, silver fish, perfectly grilled. Mom pointed to the beach, indicating it was one of the fish from the catch. *"Talk about farm to table,"* Tita Gail remarked, squirting the calamansi (similar to lemons) over the fish. Before I had time to look for a fork, my mom tore a piece of charred fish-skin with her fingers and popped it in her mouth like a French fry. The flesh was pure white and plump between my fingers. It tasted sweet, like crab. Titos and Titas, still focused on charades, passed by and picked at the fish with their fingers, as if stealing bites from a bucket of popcorn. A few more plates of grilled fish appeared in front of us. We picked, and laughed, and picked some more until all that was left on the table were plates and bones.

I had gotten it *all* wrong. It wasn't that mom had recovered enough to come on the trip. This trip *was* part of her recovery.

She was returning to a time before she gave her life to her career and her family. A time before me. There, in the land of her birth, she was not just my mother. She was not the woman who taught me how to ride the subway and weave through rush hour crowds. She was not the woman reminding me to hydrate and eat fiber. She was not the woman who disapproves of casual profanity. She was not just my mother – she was Miriam B.

In that place and time far from New York, she was the girl with wild, curly hair. She was the girl who giggled with her friend, Debbie, when they bought their first bras. *"Which were pointy, in those days!"* Tita Debbie added with a smile. She's the girl who tripped in PE class while running in the rice fields, trying to avoid stepping on a pile of carabao poo. She's the girl who skipped school with her friends to see "Grease" in theaters. *"We all got zeros on our music quiz because of that,"* Mom confessed, as she pushed a glass of water closer to me, reminding me to take a sip.

By touching base with her past, she was healing – recharging. Just like I did when I got home after kindergarten. She was getting a chance to do *that* for herself. She was also getting a chance to share that part of herself with me. The color returned to her cheeks during that trip. I just wish Papa and Daniel could have seen it for themselves.

## Tenderness

This past July, I celebrated my birthday in lockdown, like thousands of others. Jason and Mom organized a special snail mail surprise for my birthday. During the week leading up to my birthday, letters filled our mailbox from all over the world: mom's batchmates, childhood friends, neighbors, family from abroad and friends met on our travels. One by one, the letters stacked up into a pile. I moved the vase of red tulips off of my desk to make room for the stack. It was worth the wait.

I spent the morning of my birthday poring over *all* of the letters. It felt like sitting in a room and getting to catch up with each of these people. It was priceless, especially during a time when travel was not possible. I enjoyed the tactile aspect of the letters, slicing the envelopes with the letter knife, feeling the ridges of the stamps, running my fingers over the handwriting. Each letter felt like *a new kiss* for my palm.

When I think about "The Kissing Hand" now, I find it interesting that Chester was a racoon. Racoons are animals known for their tenacity. Yes, for raiding garbage and breaking into attics. But they are also excellent problem-solvers and survivors. Yet, Chester does not build strength of a physical kind, he builds emotional strength. It is not just a book about fledgling fear. It is about how *tenderness* can give us strength to confront the unknown.

A month before my birthday, I came across some letters written by the poets, Ross Gay and Noah Davis, who liked to play basketball together. In their correspondences, they talk about how tenderness underlies sport even as physically grueling as basketball. In one letter, Ross tells Noah:

> "I think it is tenderness you and I are practicing, Noey. I'm sore and bruised and bloody sometimes, my knee sounds like a pepper grinder, and my toenail's about to fall off again, but I think it's tenderness we're practicing: Some balm to the boy who would break his brother's smile. Some balm to the dad who would do the same to his son. Some sweetness to make the malice go soft. The hands for holding. The hands for tending. Some tenderness by which we kiss the broken thing in us."

Tenderness powers us as we navigate through unknown waters.

All around us, all the time, life happens. And *tenderness* endures.

*Rebecca and her husband Jason*

# REBECCA BELL

Rebecca Bell was born and raised in New York. She graduated from Hunter College with a degree in philosophy.

She enjoys hiking, dancing, and exploring new places in her renovated camper van. She now lives in San Francisco with her husband and is pursuing a career in writing.

## CHAPTER 2

# When the Wind Blows: Return to Africa

By Gloria De Guzman

I don't recall a single instance when I ever thought or dreamt of going to Africa – until I got together with two friends from my refugee camp days.

One had lived in several countries in Africa for more than two decades, while the other was leaving for her first African placement as a volunteer for Voluntary Service Overseas (VSO), a UK-based development organization.

Relatives and friends dreamt of migrating to the United States of America. So did I, but I wasn't meant to. God had other plans for me as it turned out.

Even after watching the movies "Out of Africa" and "One: the Movie" innumerable times, not once did I consider going to Africa. And yet I went in – not once, but twice…it was as if Africa called me.

My first East African assignment was Tanzania – well known for Serengeti, Lake Victoria and Zanzibar. My second

East African assignment was Uganda – well known for the Equator (zero degrees latitude, zero degrees longitude) and the Source of the Nile.

Both assignments are very memorable, and as other volunteers can attest. Volunteering placements – whether in Africa or Asia – are life-changing experiences.

A VSO contract can be short term, from three to six months; it could also be long-term, one to two years. Some volunteers stay on for about five years.

One may well ask, in what and how many ways could several months of living in a southern country for a year or longer, change a volunteer's life? The simple answer is in so many ways that I cannot begin to fathom the long-term impact.

What about our families, friends, and jobs?

In my case, I exchanged my doctoral studies for the chance to volunteer in Tanzania for two years straight. Some friends arranged send-off treats, others gave me things that I could use, and some contributed money because they knew that I would be getting a very modest allowance.

In mid-2013, I left for Tanzania with three other Filipino volunteers. I left with my family's blessing. It would be the first of three VSO placements.

After completing this assignment, my mother told me to stay put in the Philippines and return to academe. So, I found part-time jobs and taught for a year.

Then I left for my *second* VSO assignment in June 2016. It was easier convincing my mother to let me volunteer again because the project was in Cambodia. I stayed there for one and a half years.

Some months after returning, I was selected for two volunteering positions – one in Tanzania, the other in Uganda. It was a tough decision because I had been waiting for a chance to return to Tanzania, and *yet* I was being given a chance to experience living and working in another country.

It took me two weeks to tell VSO Philippines that *this* time, I wanted to go to Uganda. There was no objection from my family even if it was a long-term contract. For that I've been very thankful and have considered myself fortunate that they understood.

Africa beckoned again, and I answered its call.

In mid-August 2018, I flew back to East Africa to what would prove to be my *toughest* and *most* challenging placement.

## Karamoja

After completing my in-country orientation in the country office in Kampala, the capital of Uganda, I traveled northeast by land on a VSO vehicle with a programme officer. Based on my pre-departure research and country reality discussion with VSO staff, I knew it would take us between *nine* to *eleven* hours of travel.

The driver took a shortcut supposedly, forgoing the regular route because he picked me up quite late. We traveled through a section of the Pian-Upe Game Park and Forest Reserve. Days before, it had rained heavily. The road was heavy with mud and I held on tightly to the handrail and my belongings, because I was slipping to the left then to the right and back! At times I felt the resistance of the tires and wasn't sure if we'd *ever* reach our destination, Moroto.

I prayed hard that we wouldn't get stuck in mud for the night.

It was a very rough ride, in the dark. I kept looking for signs that we would soon be on the tarmac road the driver had mentioned. That shortcut through the game park took us almost *three hours*.

Little did I know that this would be the normal during the rainy season and that visits to the remotest schools in Karamoja were only possible during the dry season.

Later, I would soon learn that there was a prescribed time-window for trips, and as much as possible we should take the familiar route and refrain from *taking shortcuts*.

Shortcuts in Karamoja invariably resulted in *longer* travel time – because these roads were rougher and riskier. One could count the number of people using these roads with one hand and these were usually herders with their animals. Other risks included potential animal attacks, and in case of accidents, phones were useless because there was no signal there.

The Karamoja Sub-Region is made up of nine districts. The VSO Uganda Field Office in the northeast, is in Moroto.

At the time I first set foot in the district, there were only *three* tarmac roads. On my first weekend, I walked the length of those *three* roads not knowing a single word of Ngakarimojong, the local language. I also, by mistake, took a road that led to a village. It was a good thing someone told me in English that I was about to leave the town and advised me to turn back.

Each weekend thereafter, I'd set out after breakfast to explore my new environment on foot, by myself. I wanted to learn where the churches, banks, post office, market, hospital, 24/7 clinic, schools and book shops were. Each time I went around, I took note of where the other development organization offices were located. My growing list also included hotels and guest houses.

From August to October, I stayed at a hotel because the apartment unit reserved for me wasn't ready for occupancy. It would be November before I could move into a bare unit – no light bulbs, no towel rail, no curtain rods.

In addition to work responsibilities, I was also responsible for furnishing my apartment. VSO provides a modest grant to enable its volunteers to buy household items – furniture, appliances, beddings and/or kitchenware.

Because I was entering a bare unit, I ordered some necessary custom-made furniture from the best carpentry shop in the district, Naoi.

Of course, this ate up a huge chunk of my household grant, but I didn't mind because I was assured of the quality of their woodcraft. To me this spelled value for my money. The Operations Unit supported me throughout the settling-in process so I could purchase what I needed and move them into the unit.

## Lonely Weekends

To be honest, I *dreaded* Fridays. Many weekends found me feeling listless and restless – each hour seemed to stretch endlessly. At the start, Saturdays were difficult. I experienced spending several Saturdays as the *only* hotel guest.

After I'd moved into my apartment in a compound, I thought it would be much better because I'd have a few neighbors. It was *not* to be so. Many of my neighbors went home to the villages on weekends. Usually, it was just me, the two caretakers and their children who stayed in the compound.

The compound only came alive on the weekends when there was *welding*, *construction* of additional units, and *laundry* to be done. More men, women and children would be around…dogs and puppies, too. The cacophony of noises on such weekends was comforting and warming. At the very least, they were signs of life to me.

No matter how long I dragged out house chores like cleaning, washing, food-shopping, and cooking, it seemed an eternity for my watch to move from second to second, minute to minute, hour to hour.

My Sundays were structured and therefore easier to handle than Saturdays. Mornings were for attending the 7:00 am mass at Naoi – a 45-minute walk from my place, occasionally taking breakfast with the Religious of the Sacred Heart of Jesus (RSCJ) sisters and going to the outstations with them for Sunday service for the Catholic Karamojongs in far villages.

Sometimes, the sisters would invite me and Patricia, a VSO volunteer from Ireland to lunch. A few months after Patricia went back to her country, it would be me and Hilde, my Austrian neighbor, who would go with the sisters.

We were often joined by two boys dear to the hearts of the sisters, novices, aspirants and foreign guests on these Sunday outstation trips. The sisters regularly conducted home visits also – to care for people living with HIV/AIDS. At Naoi, they had established a Home-Based Care Centre and a School of Life.

To pass the other weekend hours, I read the mystery thriller pocketbooks borrowed from our Resource Room in the Kampala country. Once I had mistakenly taken a thick pocketbook of Donald Duck's adventures only to discover later that the book was in *Dutch*!

On those weekends when very few people were around, the deafening silence gave me plenty of time to reflect. It was a time for introspection.

Neil, a fellow returned volunteer, had given me a journal. So I started writing about my days. I wrote about people I interacted with, places I went as part of my volunteering work, food I ate, the dust and mud of Karamoja, *and* the plants I coaxed into surviving the merciless heat *or* the incessant rains.

I wrote small notes to myself about things I wished for, and put them into an empty coffee jar. It was like coming home to a welcoming light, one of the things I missed when I was far from home. You see, back home, my mother always left a light on whenever I taught classes until 9:00 pm, and returned home close to midnight.

In Moroto, I got so used to the dark. The sound of silence was broken only by occasional barks, bird calls, cricket sounds, motorbikes. Power was off most hours of the day, sometimes even *at night*. Water was not as much of a problem. Aside from indoor plumbing, there was a borehole across the road, where all my neighbors got their water.

Like the days, evenings also proved to be tough. During the first few weeks, I'd be in bed by 7:00 pm, reading and re-reading pocketbooks by the light of a solar lamp my mother had given me. In between chapters, I would look at *the sky* – through my sheer lace curtain – blanketed by stars. If by 10:00 pm I was still awake, I would begin counting stars…or the number of motorbikes passing – I was lucky when I could count up to five.

Oftentimes I would wake up around 2:30 a.m., unable to go back to sleep. I would wait until 5:30 am, then get up to boil water for my coffee or tea. I would sit in front of my sitting room window and sip, listening for sounds from my neighbors and waiting to see the first sunrays of a brand-new day.

Unlike in the Philippines where I and my friends *dreaded* Mondays, in Uganda I was *excited* for them.

I discovered that even if I scheduled house chores, errands, and cooking, there were still *many* hours left in a day. I was back to counting minutes and thinking of a myriad of things that could possibly keep my mind occupied.

I needed structured weekends to deal with being on my own. Hence, phone calls to family were arranged on weekend afternoons. I looked forward to hearing the voices of my mom, brother and sister, the cats meowing, the dog barking. We talked about the week and the foods we'd eaten. We talked about neighbors and family friends. These calls were my **lifeline** especially during those weekends that were particularly rough.

Sometimes my restless feet would take me to a nearby restaurant, Karamoja Tours – expensive by my standards – or to the Mount Moroto Hotel, 15-20 minutes by foot. Meals there were a bit expensive. There were two TVs, noise, a friendly dog, and people.

Weekend afternoons meant football matches – so there were quite a lot of men there cheering and jeering. Some people went there to charge their laptops and phones because the hotel had a generator. Just before dusk, I'd head home – back to my quiet world for more musings.

## Domestic headaches

There were only three windows in my apartment: one in the sitting room, one in the bedroom and the third in the bathroom. I liked leaving my windows open all day and all night, so that what little breeze there was, could come in.

I *should* have known better.

For security reasons, I spent the 2018 holidays with Julia, one of the Filipino volunteers in the Resilient Livelihoods Programme, at her apartment in Lira, a district about six hours from my place.

Those two weeks were a welcome respite for us. We spent the days walking around the town, visiting the market and supermarkets, buying a few second-hand clothes and footwear, and making pineapple jam and salted eggs.

I was given a heads-up by one of the field offices staff that Moroto had been experiencing very windy days while I was away. It was that time of year when winds were very strong, and in its wake, dust followed.

Upon my return, when I opened the door to my apartment, I braced myself. True enough, every available surface inside was covered in dust! The floor tiles, gray-green in color, were covered with red-brown dust.

Even with *all* three windows closed and the gap between the door and the floor covered with cardboard, the dust managed to come in. Cleaning the house to get rid of as much dust as is possible, took me *several* days!

To make matters worse, the strong winds continued to blow, and *nothing* I did prevented it from coming into my house.

I had to live with the fact that this was one of *several* domestic battles I could *not* win.

In 2019, the rains did *not* come in time as it did the previous year. I had thought *only the dust* would be my major headache. I was mistaken.

One night, after returning from the burial of my programme manager's father in Tororo, a district about six-seven hours away from Moroto, I entered my apartment and turned on the sitting room light. After sending SMS messages to colleagues that I had returned safely, I went to my bedroom to change. I did not turn the light on, but did leave the connecting door open to let some light in.

As I turned to change, I saw what looked like a thick, black line about two feet long on the floor, under my bedroom window and inches away from my mattress. I tried to recall if it had been there that morning because I did not remember seeing it. Silently I returned to the sitting room to get my flashlight, a gift from Patricia. I turned it on and checked this black line and found myself looking at a shiny, black snake! Thankfully, I had the presence of mind not to scream.

I closed my bedroom door and immediately went to look for Charles, one of the caretakers. I told his wife and children about the snake. Charles arrived a few minutes later. He promptly went with me, crowbar in hand.

After Charles went inside my house, I stepped out, stayed on my neighbor's porch and let Charles take care of the snake. He threw it on my porch, still writhing and wriggling, and calmly told me it was already in pain and would soon die. Perhaps because he saw that I stayed in place, he threw it further away from my porch. Mentally, I marked the spot where it landed. When morning came, it was gone.

I did not sleep on my mattress for the next two weeks. I scrunched myself into my two-seater sofa, uncomfortable but relatively safer since it was inches off the floor.

I would also make noise every time I entered my apartment and beat every box and bag with an umbrella just to be certain there were no other *uninvited* reptiles inside.

Amazingly, I did *not* fully unpack my things – it had been almost a year since I'd moved in. For some reason, I had opted to keep them in zippered sack bags and boxes – so it was *easy* to check for other snakes that may have been lurking.

Charles explained to me that snakes looked for cool places and water during the dry season.

When I told my brother about the black snake, he advised me to place onions and garlic by the door. The smell of those two *might* prevent the entry of others like it. So from then on, before I locked my door, I arranged two trays on the floor – one filled with onions, the other with garlic. My colleagues laughed at this, but I kept on doing it.

When the rains *finally* came, I rejoiced because it meant that

I would not have to clean morning, noon, and night. There would be *no* dust for some weeks – hurray!

I love the rain – it revitalized my long-suffering plants, my flowers bloomed which added spots of color in my garden and around the compound, my basil grew and multiplied fast.

I collected and stored rainwater to wash my hair with it so it would be soft and shiny again. Our tapwater was hard water, so the rains were a comfort to me.

With the rains, came *another* pressing, recurring domestic issue: it was the season of termites! They came and chose my bedroom, just like the snake. But they chose a different area. At first, it was small piles of red earth along the bottom of the wall that I could handle each day.

One morning, I noticed the termites were expanding their territory. They had crawled through the grout and advanced by several tiles! All I had were water-based insect spray and acetic acid. I poured both on the piles of red soil just before I left for the field. I thought they would be dead.

When I returned in the evening, they were back *with a vengeance*! More tiles were covered in red soil. All through the night, I couldn't sleep much, thinking of how to deal with this problem.

The following morning, I talked to Charles who promised he would call the landlord who lived in Kampala, request money to buy termite control chemicals, and purchase this in town.

Because this was Moroto, the treatment was not always available. As with many other things, the chemicals had to be brought from somewhere else. I had to wait for many days. Because the combination of insect spray and acetic acid did *not* seem to be effective, I started pouring boiling water directly on the termite mini-hills and also sprayed them each morning.

Thankfully, my ***triple action strategy*** worked long enough until eventually, Charles bought the chemicals and treated the affected areas.

## Putting down roots

In front of my apartment, the caretakers had marked off two small garden plots with slabs of marble mined from a nearby mountain. One plot was just outside my sitting room, the other outside my bedroom. Both did not have good soil. What the caretaker did was to provide me with two plant boxes, two feet long, one foot wide and one and half feet deep; these were filled with garden soil. The men placed one beneath each window. The one on the bedroom side, I planted strawberry, basil, and lemongrass.

On the ground, I planted periwinkle – white and pink – and on one corner a spider plant. The plant box on the sitting room side was planted with water spinach, lemongrass, and rosemary. On the ground I planted more periwinkles and spider plant. Many weeks later, Jethro, one of Charles's sons planted morning glory. During the rainy season, I added marigold and cherry tomatoes.

Using the big water containers I got from the field office, I requested and obtained more garden soil to plant more flowers on one side of the porch, onions and bell peppers on the other. A couple of mammillaries, taken from the sisters' garden, were each placed on the window ledges.

I wanted the butterflies and bees to come. My basil plants thrived well; in photos they resembled a foliage. I let them flourish so they would grow flowers. I collected the flowers, dried them, and gave them to my Austrian neighbor and to the sisters, to plant in their gardens.

My neighbors' children were curious about the strawberry plant. They had never seen nor tasted strawberries. So when they saw me checking on it and taking photos, they would come and ask with the little English they knew with some Kiswahili words thrown in, which I understood. When my strawberry plant grew a few flowers, I became excited. It was not easy nurturing it because of the climate.

Some weeks later, fruit started to appear – at first, they were light green, then slowly they turned bright red. Four of the five were hidden from view by the leaves. Only one was immediately visible. I would take photos morning and afternoon and share them with family and friends.

One afternoon while I was at work, the children plucked them *all* – even though the largest was only the size of my thumbnail! A neighbor saw them and told me. I would not win this challenge. It's difficult to separate children from trees and from fruit.

Gardening was my way of decompressing, de-stressing. Perhaps my neighbors wondered why I persevered in planting flowers and ornamentals while they were occupied planting maize, beans, sorghum, cassava, amaranth, sukuma wiki, cucumber, onions, tomatoes, eggplant and okra in their home gardens in the villages.

They planted these to get them through the dry season. I, on the other hand, wanted to beautify both sides of my porch. I wanted to return at the end of each workday to a profusion of colorful blooms…to remind me of home – of my mother's ornamental plants.

I also knew that growing my garden – a flower garden, no less – meant attracting bees, as well as caterpillars that would later metamorphose into butterflies and moths. Unfortunately, these *also* attracted *nasty* reptiles.

But being a foreigner and outsider meant that I needed to create a haven *for myself*. I wanted to "go home" at the end of each work day to a cheery house, one that I'd always look forward to seeing, photographing and sharing with family and friends. To show that my plants were healthy, thriving in a land that could be harsh and brutal. It was an oasis. A small one, but an oasis, nonetheless.

I was also aware that as my garden thrived, I was also symbolically *putting down roots*. I knew that when my contract ended, it would be hard to leave the place I had temporarily called home.

On the bright side, though, whoever would occupy that apartment after I left would have a cheerful place to go home to. He, she or they would feel welcome. Perhaps they would enjoy eating the strawberries and cherry tomatoes, harvesting the onions and bell peppers. They might also enjoy spicing up their tea with my lemongrass!

Surprisingly, I was the only tenant in the compound who planted a garden. The sight of my garden soothed my frayed nerves and calmed my occasionally-anxious heart. I only hoped that the plants I lovingly cultivated would survive the dry spell.

## Simple cooking

For those of us in the field, a day's work meant we had *little* energy left to make ourselves a nutritious meal. In both my African placements, the egg was a lifesaver. I made omelets – sometimes plain, sometimes with onions, sometimes with tomatoes, sometimes with potatoes, sometimes with green bell pepper. Cheese could only be bought in the capital, so I rarely made cheesy omelets. A few times, I made a basic shakshouka – an egg dish of North African origin, and an egg salad. Often for breakfast, I had soft-boiled eggs. When I was in the mood for instant noodles, I would add an egg.

One couldn't buy a gas canister in my district, or in the

next. The nearest place was about *three and a half hours* away by private vehicle. If I'd run out of gas, I would have to wait till an office vehicle was scheduled to go to the capital or the next region. This could take days! This meant that I had to be judicious in using up my gas.

Since I could live without eating meat for long periods, I mostly cooked vegetable and pasta dishes. To further reduce cooking time and save on gas, I shifted to one-pot pasta meals that didn't take long to cook. By looking up recipes online, I discovered *pasta alla norma* and *pasta e patate*. I tweaked both recipes because there were ingredients that were available only in Kampala and not easily affordable to volunteers.

## Pet friendly

I befriended my neighbors' dogs. To them they were merely guard dogs; to me, they were more than that.

I learned their names and often spent some minutes talking to them and playing with them: Barack, Freshian, Scooby, Coco, and Tiger.

I'd place two basins under the waterspouts on my porch to collect rain water. The dogs would drink from these. During the dry months, I would leave tap water in the basins outside by my door.

When Freshian gave birth to three puppies, I gave them milk to drink. I showed the children in the compound how to hold them, how to carry them. Occasionally, in the middle of the night I would be awakened by slurping sounds. It was the dogs coming to my place for water! It was comforting to hear those sounds. So I made it a point to leave water in a basin for them.

## Christened

On 14 October 2018, a Sunday, Sisters Paulina and Margie, along with five-year old Edison (a boy who aspires to be a driver and catechist) and two girls, took me to Nakiloro, a village near the Kenyan border, about 45 minutes from town. The sisters wanted to lend me a shawl because it could get very cold in that village. I told them I had one in my bag; I had just bought it from a second-hand shop across from the hotel.

When we reached Nakiloro, the sisters proudly showed me "the church". It was a shade tree and under its sprawling branches – which also served as a roof – were benches made from tree trunks arranged in a half-moon shape. It was an open area, within the property of the village dispensary. It was pleasantly cool under the shade of the tree. The service was led by Moses, a cathechist, and Sister Paulina. The mass was said in Ngakarimojong, my first time to hear mass in the regional language. Sr. Paulina speaks it very fluently.

After the mass, I was introduced to the congregation. I was also given a Karamojong name. Sr. Paulina thought of one and said it softly, but it was Sabina, one of the female elders, who said it out loud. The rest agreed with the choice.

Names are assigned based on the first visit to the village, and could be based on the weather or prevailing activity, such as in the case of the sisters. Sr. Paulina was named **Nakiru**, meaning *rain*, because it was raining when she first set foot in the village. Sr. Margie, on the other hand, was named Amot, because she first visited them when the people were busy making clay pots.

It was windy that day, and this was why I was bestowed the name, **Nakut**, meaning *wind*. This was a significant moment for me because it was the first time I had been assigned a local name! In my previous VSO placements, I was merely given the translations of my first name.

## Together we can

One Sunday, I went with Sr. Paulina and Sr. Margie to a chapel built by the Germans. The road there was bad...it's worse in the rainy season. Midway, our vehicle got stuck, so we had to walk all the way to the chapel. People had been waiting for us and for mass to start.

Just before we left the chapel, Sr. Paulina requested the people to help us cover the ground with stones and rocks. Under the heat of the merciless noontime sun, there was work to be done. There were a few men, more women, and girls. There was no wheelbarrow so we only used our hands and heads. Even the older Karamojong women came to help.

The place where we left our vehicle was near a quarry. People, with the exception of the two octogenarian sisters, carried slabs of marble and rocks. Despite suffering from de Quervain's tenosynovitis, I was able to carry several slabs. Girls carried 5-7 slabs on their heads! Imagine how strong their necks must have been be to carry such heavy loads! With everyone helping – men, women and children – we managed to fill in the deep, dangerous gaps on the road and made it safe for others. The road was temporarily improved for everyone going to Musupo.

Together we did it.

## Do no harm

One evening, I had two visitors whom I'd never met before. The older person asked me for a huge favor – to give the teenaged girl shelter. Her rescuer requested one night's shelter. And yet this posed several complications – to the rescuer, the teenager, myself as volunteer, my organization, and my neighbors. I only knew of the rescuer and his work through colleagues who occasionally visited his area.

The girl had knocked on their office door for help. I didn't know all the facts that led to her decision…only that she was escaping from an arranged marriage and was determined to get herself an education so she could have a better future. A rational solution, not one solely based on emotions.

What was plain was that she wasn't going back to her village, and she wanted a say in her future. What did she want? An education. To finish her studies so she could get out of poverty. To know another world, a brighter world – one without poverty. That is what she wanted – what many other Karamojong girls want.

She remarkably didn't appear agitated. I couldn't even imagine how she felt about **not** having *anyone* else to turn to nor trust among her relatives and friends.

How brave of her to go against cultural norms and practices. Brave enough to escape from her village, walk for who-knows-how-long, knock on her rescuer's door and ask for help!

She had exceptional courage – the courage and determination to complete her education. The courage to leave her family and everything else she knew and was familiar with, to build a better future for herself. She certainly wanted *more* out of life. It must not have been easy for her.

I don't even want to think if she had already undergone female genital mutilation, a cultural practice that continues in the region. The rescuer and his colleagues had saved many girls from this culturally-backed practice. As a result of their rescue work, they had received countless death threats.

Due to the lateness of the hour, there wasn't much I could do for this teenager. I was bound by organizational policy on safeguarding; I had signed a document. I was incredibly torn between acceding to the request versus following organizational policy.

Reason over emotion prevailed. All I could do was refer the rescuer to a religious person whom I knew had an extra bed, could protect the teenager, provide a sanctuary, and a safe haven for the night. The rescuer understood my situation; he had worked with many development organizations and was familiar with policies and restrictions.

I do not know what happened after they left my apartment. I never saw the rescuer again. I can only pray that the teenager is in safe hands, and is able to complete her education. I didn't speak of this singular incident with anyone.

For many weeks thereafter I lived with the uncertainty of whether I had done the right thing – if I should've given that girl shelter for a night. What was a few hours? Yet in those few hours, anything could've happened. Her relatives and those of her would-be husband could've discovered where she was hiding. The consequences could've been *more dire* if **warriors** were involved. I did not speak about the incident to any colleague at work. But I did mention it to one of the sisters in the parish. She conveyed that had they been around, they could have sheltered her for a night, but no more.

Time was of the essence when rescuing these girls. They'd have to be moved out of the region the soonest possible, far away from their relatives, out of harm's way, in a safe haven. That girl put her life into her rescuer's hands. He and his colleagues risked their lives to help her.

After several weeks passed, I attended a workshop by our safeguarding specialist. I asked her about my decision, and she assured me that I made the right decision and shouldn't feel guilty. It was the affirmation I needed. Yes, it was difficult to make but it was the *right* one. No one knows what would've happened had I sheltered the girl and how that *one* incident would've ended.

A friend, who also worked for a development organization, was also asked to help by one of her staff. In this instance, it was a case of domestic violence. She, too, was restricted by guidelines.

So we asked around – about local NGOs (Non-Government Organizations) that focused their work on domestic violence and gender-based violence – which were in a much better position to help. My friend was able to refer the matter to the head of a local NGO. The most that we could do was tap into our network of friends and colleagues, to seek advice, and refer. This was the only action we could take. We couldn't get involved. We weren't from there and didn't fully know the system.

As development workers, we're also called to keep a tight rein on our emotions, remain steadfast, think quickly on our feet, assess the risks *and* evaluate based on facts we know. We had to make sensible decisions, not ones that tugged on our heart strings.

## Circular

Almost every morning, on my way to the field office, primary pupils walked alongside or behind me. Sometimes, a few would run ahead and look back at me. Often, they would speak in gibberish – they probably thought I was Chinese.

I decided to ignore the Chinese references and their *"Mzungu, good morning! How are you?"* greetings. Whenever they greeted me that way, I'd respond quickly in broken Kiswahili with, *"Mzungu??? Eeee, wapi? Kuingia, siona; kulia, siona. Sema, mzunguwapi?"*, complete with theatrical movements! They'd all start guffawing!

Once the ice was broken, I'd start a conversation with them. Frequently I'd ask them if they were happy in school. They'd respond *"Yes!"*

My next question was, *"Why?"* Answers invariably were, *"Because I learn."* I'd probe, *"What do you learn in school?"* They'd respond with, *"To read."*

I'd ask, *"What do you like to read in school?"* To this, the answers varied.

Some said they read English, others Science, others Math.

I'd probe further, asking my favorite question, *"Why do you like to read _____?"* The answer was, *"Because I like _____."* To which I'd say, *"Yes, you said that earlier, but why? What is it about ____ that you like?"* The answer could go, *"Because it makes us happy."* Hmmm, so we'd end up with my original question. I'd start over, *"Why are you happy?"* The children gamely went along with me and replied, *"Because we read."* *"And what do you read?"* *"We read English, Science and Math."* *"And what do you read in English, Science and Math?"* *"We read books."* *"In those books, what do you read?"* Then the children would start laughing. Once we'd reached the fork in the road, we'd wish each other a pleasant day.

All I could do to make them forget their circumstances even for a few moments was to wheedle smiles, giggles or laughter from each of them. I did everything including making a fool of myself on the road because once they'd hear me speak, they'd start laughing! They'd laugh at my accent because the children thought I was from China. They imitated the way I spoke; their imitation was always nasal which made me wonder why to them I sounded nasal and not sibilant.

I reminded myself that there might be other days when I just might get through to them. I wanted to know what it was about school that made them happy. Their answers would confirm to us – VSO, UNICEF, DEO – that schools were making *some* headway.

I think that if children are happy in school, then they must feel safe there.

## Akoror

On weekdays, I met and had quick exchanges with children going to school. Often, they greeted me first with, *"Mzungu, good morning. How are you?"* Sometimes, I reminded them **not** to call me mzungu. When I did, they quickly referred to me as "sister".

What profoundly affected me, though, was that some of them did not have shoes nor slippers. Once I asked a boy where his slippers were and he told me quietly, *"They are not there."* I knew better than to ask a follow-up question or to ask another boy, or girl, the same question. I knew about pride. I had to be content that they continued to attend their classes.

As a volunteer for another UNICEF-funded project, I came face-to-face with poverty on a daily basis. The poverty I constantly faced was of *two* kinds: poverty of the stomach and poverty of the mind.

On field visits, I felt helpless whenever I saw school-aged boys, out in the wide, harsh bush land. Instead of studying, they were out in the middle of nowhere, walking *endless miles* through savannahs behind their herds of cows and calves, sheep and lambs, goats and kids, under the *scorching* heat of a merciless sun.

These boys traveled armed only with a *shuka* (Massai blanket) and a stick. When the boys went hungry, they drank straight from a milking cow, or a lactating sheep or goat; but this hinged on the availability of water. If the cows, sheep, and goats didn't drink, then there was definitely no milk for the boys either.

I silently wept whenever I saw school-aged girls walking on the roadside balancing on their heads bundles of firewood, sacks of charcoal or 20-liter jerry cans containing water. Some of them gathered tree branches and long grass so they could hire themselves out to construct *manyattas*, a group of traditional huts. Some of them were out in the fields to plant, weed and harvest. Sometimes I'd see only *one* teenaged girl working in the field; it would be many more kilometers before I'd see another person.

In town, it was common to see children who walked to school wearing threadbare, ill-fitting clothes, clutching black *kaveras* (plastic bags) often containing a plastic cup, a plate or a reusable margarine container, as well as torn, old books.

Many of them walked barefoot to school. They stepped on dung, spit, phlegm, glass shards, rough stones – rain or shine. I wondered if their feet felt *anything* at all.

Whenever I met children who wanted to hold my hand, touch my arm, *or* stroke my hair, I didn't see grimy hands. I saw shy smiles, happy faces. I didn't even spare a second to think whether or not they were HIV-positive. I only felt *their* need to know joy in their young lives. Even for just a fleeting moment.

Some of these children came from homes that knew only *violence*, never love. They knew what it was like to do *without* – without water, without food, without clothes, without parents, without medicine. Without books.

My eyes have seen a poverty that has silenced my tongue on many occasions. Inside, I'd weep as my heart bled. Outside, I appeared *unfazed*, allowing the children to see only a bright, cheery countenance.

I know very little Ngakarimojong and some Kiswahili but with a little bit of drama and exaggerated gestures and expressions, I was able to make these children laugh – *at* me and *at themselves*. Once the silence was broken, by peal after peal of their heartfelt laughter, I felt better. In those few, fleeting moments, their world was transformed into one that resonated with *pure joy*.

Then and there, I glimpsed hope. For this world.

To this day, six months after I and all other international volunteers in Uganda were repatriated because of the pandemic, I continue to miss the wide, open spaces of Africa. I miss seeing the raw beauty of the African bush. I miss travelling through rough, dusty roads on sunny days, and getting through flooded back roads, dangerous mud and roads overgrown with tall grasses on rainy days. I miss looking at an unhindered view of the night sky – the stars appearing brighter and cheerier. I miss walking alongside herds. I even miss being asked, *"Mzungu, how are you?"*

I miss being called **Nakut** by my colleagues. I miss Africa. **Mungu akipenda, ninarudi Africa.**

L →R: Gloria's sister Glenda, brother
Gabriel, Gloria, and their mother Placida

## Gloria De Guzman

Gloria de Guzman is a licensed professional teacher. She earned her Bachelor of Arts in Humanities (Pre-Medicine) and Master of Arts in Asian Studies from the University of the Philippines, Diliman; she obtained her Certificate in Professional Education from the Laguna Polytechnic State College. She was in academe for many years: University of the Philippines Los Baños, University of the Philippines Open University, De La Salle University Manila, College of St. Benilde and Asia Pacific College. She taught humanities, world and Philippine literature, research writing, advanced and basic technical writing, public speaking, English grammar, and Asian history. She also taught English as a Second Language (ESL) with the International Catholic Migration Commission (ICMC) and later the International Social Service (ISS) at the Philippine Refugee Processing Center in Morong, Bataan.

Gloria was a volunteer faculty supervisor of an all-female team for the Affirmative Action Program of the Ugnayan ng Pahinungod, University of the Philippines Los Baños. She, along with one Math instructor and four undergraduate students, were assigned to Parang, Maguindanao in April

1996 to prepare 30 graduating students to take the University of the Philippines College Admission Test (UPCAT).

In mid-2013, Gloria left the academe to venture into international development work with Voluntary Service Overseas (VSO), a UK-based development organization. Since then she has taken up three placements as an education volunteer: as a Leadership Facilitator for the DFID-funded EQUIP-T ELT Project in Tanzania (2013-15), as an Education Management Adviser for the UNICEF-funded SEM Project in Cambodia (2016-2017) and as the Materials Development and Teacher Training Adviser for the UNICEF/Irish Aid-funded A PLUS Project in Uganda (2018-2020). At present, Gloria continues to support the A PLUS Project but as a remote volunteer; she was repatriated in late March because of the COVID-19 pandemic. She is also part of the Voluntary Workforce of VSO.

# CHAPTER 3
# Sunshine Boy
By Miriam De Leon, M.D.

## Unexpected Angels

Dear Nathan,

I can close my eyes and remember the moment you stopped looking at me. It broke my heart.

I can feel that imaginary thud in my gut that told me something was very wrong. But, to manage the panic, I started creating stories in my head. Stories that made it easier—to do what exactly, I wasn't sure, but it felt more manageable at the time. Stories like "It's just a phase." "Boys develop slower than girls." "Each baby is different." Somehow even with my medical education, I believed these stories, because believing them was easier than the inevitable alternative.

If there is one thing that I learned from my hospital rotations, it's that it is a good thing to have nurses on your side. Dr. Wolfe was your neurologist and had decided to admit you to the epilepsy monitoring unit. Even with wires attached to your head you were our adorable little boy. "Just for a few days." He said. Then we can find out what is causing those episodes. At that time the episodes were short almost in a staccato rhythm.

Your short arms would flail up in the air and your face would grimace almost in a momentary strain. They came in clusters of 4 or 5 at a time. On the second morning I called the nurses' station to ask about the night. Somehow, the way the nurse said, "Oh hi!" on the phone made me swallow harder. "You found something?" I asked.

I pushed the heavy double doors into the unit and walked what seemed like miles to the nurses' desk. Rows of screens lined the wall one for each bed. In a very familiar Filipino accent, she said, "I've seen a lot of these in my years….but the doctor will be in shortly to speak to you and your husband."

I had read about infantile spasms only fleetingly in med school. Dr. Wolfe was very gentle. My head was swimming with phrases like "undetermined brain damage", "developmental delays "and early intervention". I immediately went into Marine-like mommy mode of: "OK, what can be done? Like now?"

Harder words and phrases followed, worst of all was this: "worldwide shortage" referring to ACTH, the injectable drug of choice for your seizures at that time. Your Papa and I felt utterly helpless.

One of your angels came in the form of a mild-mannered Jewish man with a naughty smile and a shock of white hair.

"Come in Miriam!" he said. "I was told you have a problem." I hesitated at first. After all, it's not every day that one is called to the office of the head of your organization. After I tearfully explained your need, he lightly patted my shoulder and said, "Don't cry, we will see what we can do."

The next day his secretary called for me to come upstairs. "He's away for a conference but gave strict instructions for you to go inside his office."

I took such measured steps into what felt like an inner sanctum. The plush carpet with a swirly pattern smelled freshly vacuumed. My eyes rose upward and fell upon on a tall, brown paper bag looking out of place on top of a glistening wooden desk as imposing as the owner. There was no note.

To this day, I will never know how a one-month supply of your medication ended up in that paper bag. But your father and I will forever be grateful.

The steroid made you plump and ravenous. But the seizures were held at bay for a while. Celebrating small victories became a constant and relentless life lesson that we needed to learn over and over and over again.

What followed was a roller coaster ride of doctors, therapists, scans and medications.

Many angels followed. Caregivers from near and far. There was a prayer I would say, asking God to bless and prepare all those who would be coming into our lives to help us and help you navigate through your journey.

I still say that prayer…every day.

## Sleepless Nights

You were two when the night terrors began. Something happens to a mother's sleep-wakefulness cycle when she is constantly waiting for her precious baby boy to wake up with a violent start followed by inconsolable crying and wailing. For *hours*. For *years*.

That cycle was put on pause, and just as well. Looking back, it felt like it was a "group" diagnosis that applied to the whole household. I will never forget one such night in a string of similar nights. Not only were you having an episode, you were also hungry. Like a zombie I stumbled in the dark to prepare your bottle when a small voice said calmly: "That's OK Mommy, I'll take care of him, you go to sleep."

In utter awe, I watched as your sister, just a little over three at the time, took over with a very grown up serenity and decisiveness. Right then I knew that she would be an angel to you, and to the family.

Just when we thought the seizures were gone, came another wave. Bigger, longer. This time, your whole body shook for seconds that seemed like forever. The force was so great that transient pinpoint hemorrhages showed up on your face. Your prolonged empty staring into space and heavy sleepiness became regular post-seizure expectations. I had an almost robotic protocol: intramuscular injection of Ativan, the obligatory 911 call and the call to Dr. Wolfe, the trip to the ER.

I had his schedule memorized so I could tell which number to call depending on the day. "Wednesdays, St. John's hospital. Thursdays, White Plains. Monday and Friday mornings, his office in Dobbs Ferry."

Very reluctantly, Papa had to learn to give you the injections himself. Firmly holding his hand around the syringe, I said " In case, something happens to me…" I hesitated, "you need to know how to do this," as we pushed the long needle into your thigh. We had to keep track of which side we stuck so we could alternate each time.

Each time, we were painfully aware that with every oxygen-starved second, your brain was suffering some *undetermined* kind of damage. "Undetermined" is such a cruel word. Translation: "we won't know until later." This meant waiting. And waiting.

But it also meant that we as a family had to learn to be gracious in receiving the love and help from those around us. Papa Joe, our next-door neighbor, went from leaving his lawn mower by our front porch as a not-too-subtle hint, to actually cutting the grass himself. My coworkers had a grocery run organized every week. These and more were examples of God's Love personified, very real daily reminders that everything required for your care was "included" in this awesome package. Yes, even the toilet paper.

My early training as an E.R. doctor was soon to be put to the test. "M-A-R-Y-A-M!!!!" was the shrill call I heard from the upstairs bedroom. As fast as I could, I ran up to find Helen, your caregiver, flailing her arms wildly, she had opened all the windows and turned on all the lights. I scooped you up from our bed. You were limp in my embrace, your body blue, lips even bluer.

I remember the 4-minute ambulance ride to the hospital that first time. And the second.

Even if only to have successfully revived you both times, I have a sure peace that all of my medical training was part of the plan.

Things *did* eventually quiet down. Ambulance trips went down from 3 a week to 2, to none. Now we could focus our energies into what was "undetermined".

To help you along in your development, an army of therapists came to give you early intervention. Our house had a revolving door. My desk calendar wonderfully color-coded to keep track of all the comings and goings.

We also had a song for *everything*: sitting, walking, popping bubbles, eating, and all the other seemingly ordinary tasks that can so easily be taken for granted.

Your Papa was particularly **relentless** in teaching you how to walk. He would prop your feet on top of his own and move one foot first and then the other while singing this catchy "walking" song. "He **has** to walk! He will miss **so** much if he stays in a wheelchair!" He was laser-focused on this mission. One day, you walked on your own! Tears. Celebration. You were five.

After you took those first steps, there was no stopping you. With the balance of a mountain goat you would scale the steep steps of our old colonial staircase but OUTSIDE the banister! You especially enjoyed climbing to the highest point in any room. That meant cabinets, dressers, and *boulders* in Central Park. You would squeal in unadulterated glee when you had the whole family scrambling in your version of "Catch me if you can".

At this point it became evident that I had a time sensitive choice to make. I could pursue my medical career or dive in with everything I had, into raising my family. I felt it a gift to have a "back up" career in physical therapy that would allow me the flexibility to enjoy a fulfilling occupation and still be very much the wife and mother I worked on becoming. Your Papa would make a similar decision a few years later, leaving a booming career in IT to work closer to home with a more predictable schedule.

Not everyone understood, of course, and we had to endure ridicule even from those we held near and dear. Success as it turned out meant different things to different people. For us, your parents, the priority was to raise our children as best we could, ourselves. We were determined to give you a home and an unwavering sense of family. Whatever the cost. Is this not what every parent strives for? When priorities are well defined, choices, though tough, are simple. Adjustments are made where they are needed.

## Faucets and Doors

There were relatively quiet four or five years until you discovered faucets and doors. To this day, most doors in our house, bathrooms included, can only be locked from the outside as this allowed us to let you wander on your own safely. We never bothered to take down the bolts.

It was a typical Friday night. After dinner, washed and pajama-ed up, you settled in your bed. We retreated downstairs to the den. I can't remember what movie we were watching, but I know that it was the last suspenseful few minutes when I felt a drop of something on my head. Then another. And another. I looked up and saw the ominous beads of water on the ceiling.

Yelling and jumping at the same time, it was indeed a miracle that we all got out of the way of a good square foot and a half of the ceiling falling right on top of us! You had discovered the delight of overfilling the upstairs bathtub with hot water. What mattered was that no one was hurt. The exact scene would happen again the following year.

Call it an occupational predisposition to thinking about "worst case" planning. I did not say anything to the family because it was difficult and painful to admit that perhaps even with the best of intentions and all the love in our hearts, the day would come when we could no longer keep you safe in your own home.

It was another Friday night. You in bed. Us in the family room. Or so we thought. I remember it was late, close to ten o'clock when the doorbell rang. "Strange," I thought as I walked to the door. Like partial Polaroid shots, I can tell you there was an old red sedan parked in the middle of the intersection across our house. Curiously, all 4 doors were swung wide open. As if in slow motion my eyes fell upon a pair of dirty sneakers and a pair of dirty blue jeans, but I cannot remember a face. "Good evening, Ma'am," said the voice that was near and distant at the same time. "Does he belong to you?" And there you were, next to this stranger, in your blue pajamas with the small cars. "Nathan!!!!" I screamed as I grabbed you. In the time it took your father, sister and younger brother to run to the front door, the man and the red car were gone. Goosebumps. Each time I tell this story. Each time.

## The Move

These and a few other heart-stopping events later, it became quite clear that you needed more supervision than we could provide. Site visits and mounds of paperwork. You were sixteen when you moved into a residential school 20 minutes away.

How many times can a mother's heart be broken? As many as it takes.

That was ten years ago.

"Nathan! Your family is here!" You ran to the backyard of your group home on Long Island. Grabbing our hands, our necks and vocalizing excitedly as if to say "Guys!! What took you so long?" It was our first visit since the 2020 lockdown. Five months, we had to sing to you through FaceTime, tell you stories of home and send love from uncles, aunties, and friends.

During that visit, you loved roaming around while your brother played "Fly Me To the Moon" on his ukulele, sharing french fries with us on the swing, your sister on the phone from San Francisco. Never mind that you cannot talk with words, your voice and your smile fill us up just as much. Just like sunshine, we cannot imagine our lives without you. We will always be here for you as you are for us. We'll be back to visit very soon.

With all the love in the world,

*Mom*

*Miriam and Nathan*

*Miriam, Nathan and Frank*

*2nd row: Miriam, her husband Frank, son Daniel*
*1st row: Daughter Becky, Nathan and Jason (Becky's husband)*

# Miriam De Leon, M.D.

Miriam Grace B. De Leon was born and raised in Manila, Philippines. Attended University of the Philippines High School.

She got her degree in Physical Therapy from the University of the Philippines School of Allied Medical Professions, where she taught for 2 years before going to the Pamantasan ng Lungsod ng Maynila College of Medicine where she finished her medical degree in 1989.

She lives in New York with her husband Frank and their Labradoodle Mindy. They have 3 children: Rebecca, Nathan and Daniel. She loves musical theater, cooking and dogs.

## CHAPTER 4

# Not Without Tears

By Leni Hufana-Del Prado

### Relentless Courage

*"Courage is to feel the daily daggers of Relentless steel and keep on living."*

~Douglas Malloch

What would you do if your life is marked with afflictions and misfortunes?

Daily daggers, wounds, desperation can be a driving force in searching for the One Thing that will give us tranquility.

At fifty-eight years old, I have come to meet some inspiring women, many of them have become dear friends of mine and not just acquaintances.

These are women who live *authentic* lives. They are not embarrassed to share their failures and wrong decisions. They expose themselves in a way that is humbling and yet they suffer in silence.

They don't force anyone to come to their aid, nor do they demand for anyone's attention to help them but they ask for prayers, not from everyone but from a few women who will genuinely pray for them.

I have come to know Marie (withholding her full name for confidentiality).

She is a woman that's easy to please and easy to love as she is soft-spoken, meek and yet full of wisdom. The harshness of life is etched in her beautiful facial features and her eyes bear a tenderness that's *rarely* seen in someone who has suffered much.

Her authenticity comes from a deep reverence for God. Most of her life was built on journeys through multiple storms of life.

While she recalls her childhood, she has to come to grips with its reality and the accompanying intense emotions. She calmly relates her past and I'm deeply grateful to her that I have been privy to her life and her struggles.

Marie is the fourth child of a brood of nine children with what people would call a good-for-nothing father. She grew up in a home with a jobless, drunk, womanizing father and a simple housewife for a mother.

Her grandfather who was a U.S. veteran sent some support for schooling which wasn't enough for their big family.

Because Marie's family lived in poverty, she was separated from her siblings and moved in with her Aunt.

I picture a family living in a cramped place, with the scarcity of basic necessities and having to witness a selfish dad who always had a bottle of beer and a woman on-the-side with a mother who tolerated the adulterous relationship.

Hardships and poverty in conjunction with difficult circumstances and difficult people were what Marie's life was like. Whenever I listened to her stories, I felt as if I were in the middle of a boxing ring taking all the blows and trying so hard to hit back, yet always missing that one big jab to the jaw that would send the opponent tumbling.

Her Aunt wasn't easy to live with either. She was harsh. Marie was slapped, pinched, and beaten for simple mistakes! She was constantly left alone.

She only had a handful of friends and there wasn't anyone to help her do homework and projects, nor anyone to talk with at the end of a hectic day.

She was also treated like a maid at such a tender age of eight and was sent to the market to buy produce. Yes, school tuition fees were paid for by her aunt – but in reality, she paid for them through hard work and beatings.

It was very difficult growing up under the umbrella of a Nazi-like officer, disguised as her aunt. It was grueling and exhausting!

Marie hardly had time to rest and play with the handful of friends that she had. While watching her friends enjoying a carefree life, her only form of entertainment was looking outside of the window and daydream. It was an escape from the hostile environment of home.

This reminds me of Cosette in the musical "Les Miserable". Before she was taken under the wing of a kind gentleman Jean Valjean, she was in a toxic environment very similar to that of Marie's.

She escaped the harsh reality of her life by dreaming of a castle on a hill.

Marie grew up a loner and people took advantage of her naiveté. A relative of hers tried to molest her. And while fetching water at a nearby place, a *close friend of her aunt* tried the same disgusting behavior on her, when she was at the tender age of ten! It is so appalling! Indeed, she walked on a path of austerity and hardship.

In contrast, the only adversities I ever faced as a young girl were a bully for a neighbor, and the rigidity of a teacher.

One expects to be raised in a home of unconditional love, acceptance, and peace. I grew up in the school of hard knocks myself. My mom was strict, and we didn't grow up with wealth, but home was a safety net that my sisters and I ran to when the environment outside the home was tough.

Marie *didn't* have that safe environment which was crucial for any child to develop security and self-respect.

Each time she would make a mistake, she was severely punished. She wasn't praised for a job well done, nor did she ever experience a tight squeeze of affection from her parents.

She didn't have those special times at the dinner table chatting, giggling, laughing with her parents and siblings, nor experience being tucked in bed by her dad or praying together as a family. She had none of those...yet, I see a peaceful disposition.

Something must have happened to her that *didn't* make her a bitter fifty-five-year-old. Instead, she exudes a gentle spirit and beauty from within.

During her teen years, she was teased frequently because she was different from all the other teens especially in the way she dressed.

While other teens would follow the latest trend in hairstyles and fashion, she didn't have the luxury of being fashionably adept. She didn't have time to think about such frivolous things because her survival instincts occupied her thoughts.

Each day was an ordeal living with her aunt, and she had to deal with a maniac of a grandfather. At eighteen, she was a looker. Her facial features were a standout with her doe eyes and high cheekbones. These assets combined with a meek spirit were probably what attracted men to her.

She was naïve to the wiles of the world, yet she needn't leave home to be sexually assaulted. Her incestuous, predator grandfather used to touch her inappropriately, and even came short of raping her!

I've heard stories of sexual predators and it makes me loathe these dirty, old men who take advantage of the innocent and helpless. I've read that it is normal for victims to suffer in silence since they feel threatened and intimidated by the offender.

Afraid to fight back and run to the police, she decided to run away from home for self-protection. She missed her exams in school, so when she showed up at school, the dean sensed that there was something dark happening behind her expressionless stare and somber demeanor.

It was understandably difficult for her to open up since she was sexually violated but she broke her silence. The school threatened to sue him and expose him as a sexual predator.

She refused out of fear to be labeled a liar because in this case, the offender was influential in their neighborhood and she would only be exposed to ridicule. I could see the sting still etched in her expressions as she recounted her story. I felt that I might have pressed her too much by asking hard questions.

The aftermath of repeated sexual violation is traumatizing. There is a feeling of self-blame, believing that you're 'damaged goods' and an oppressive blanket of shame.

It usually takes a long time for one to heal…even nightmares and flashbacks occur. She hopped from one friend to another, hoping that she would have rest from her trauma. Like every woman, she too hoped that someday she would have a grand house of her own with the love of her life beside her.

It was very challenging for Marie to recall the most agonizing parts of her broken past because she had renounced it and surrendered it to God. I thanked her for allowing me to probe. I may have opened old wounds that she would've rather forgotten.

She had met someone who pursued her. John (not his real name) *wasn't* handsome in a conventional way but had an animal magnetism and an appeal that women were attracted to. She gave herself *totally* to him, both body and soul.

After a year, they got married and soon had their first born. Then another daughter was born soon after.

It was early in their marriage when the *terrible news* hit her like a bolt of lightning: John had other marriages prior to theirs which rendered her marriage *null and void! This* shattered the very core of her being.

She also discovered that he had several affairs even while they were married! Women would flirt with him even in her presence. There was even a time when Marie received a call from one of his mistresses telling her to remind her (Marie's) husband that she was waiting for him in the hotel room!

I tried to visualize Marie's reaction while those incidents were happening. Marie is a tenderhearted person. I have difficulty trying to picture that scene with Marie having a fit or confronting the women using vulgar language. She didn't want to relive those heart-breaking moments. It was too much for her and I completely understood.

Being the survivor that she is, even with a despairing heart and wounded spirit, she soldiered on. She carried the burden while thinking of the welfare of her daughters. But her tolerance had reached its limit.

Courageous women who have been abused and disrespected by their own man, shake the dust off their feet, leaves and don't look back.

Marie knew that starting over would mean a back-breaking journey. She didn't know how they were going to make it, but she mustered all the courage she had stored in her, and took it upon herself to get up and get on with her life. Thankfully, she had the strength of character to be keep her sanity and move on.

Marie packed up and left with *five* kids in tow, and a *sixth* on the way!

How was she able to get back on her feet? How did she cope with caring for six children? It would've left me baffled had I *not* known her tenacity. She brought this same resolve with her *through to the next years* of her life.

She didn't balk at the process of owning up to her failures, nor did she balk at her commitment to raise her *six* daughters *on her own*.

Her fear did not impede any plans to look for a job. She spent days, scouring the city's business district looking for a job on foot. After walking for several hours, she finally found a job at a gentleman's club in the middle of the vibrant city that was swarming with Manila's elite.

It was a private social club set up for men from the upper class. She was hired as a receptionist and a floor manager to oversee the staff and check the stock in the kitchen and bar.

Her major role, however, was to offer the young ladies to the male clients. She was stunned and shell-shocked at first because she wasn't used to this way of life. She empathized with those young ladies…but she figured that they needed to make a living. Besides, at the end of their shifts, their boyfriends would pick them up.

Even if it didn't make any sense to her then, she just saw that lifestyle as the norm. In addition to that, her daughters' needs came above her own. She couldn't afford to lose her job, and it wasn't her place to question authority nor rebuke them.

Her family was banking on her to be both the father and mother of their home. But she would clock off at three in the morning in time to take care of her children. Exhausted from the work hours and unhealthy environment, she opted to look another job that gave her more flexibility and time with her children.

She was able to find a job as a Dining Manager in charge of the day to day operations and activities inside the restaurant. It was her answer to rise from poverty. She was well paid and received generous tips from customers. She stayed with them for four years.

It was only when she was continually belittled, harassed by

the boss' wife and her mean peers – out of spite – that she decided it was time to move on.

In all the years I've known Marie, I can confidently share that she's not the kind of woman that flirts around nor was she the kind of woman that played with fire. She's smart and sacrificial in her love for her children. She was the heroine of her six daughters and in her poverty, she managed to raise *all* of them without the help of any man.

She was hard working and *didn't* give any reason for any woman to feel insecure or envious of her. Maybe it was her beautiful smile, or the modest way she walked, or it could be the gentleness of her voice.

She's the kind of woman who is unassuming in her ways and didn't really take time to care much about herself. She didn't live in a world with superimposed standards that were shared by many. She was conservative in her dress and decent in her ways. She was highly respected by the clients and her boss.

She continued working in the restaurant business, not yielding to any distraction, just walking the straight and narrow path. Yet it seemed that the saying 'misfortunes tend to follow one another in accelerated succession' was true for her.

In 2008, she lost her job. Her son had to stop school because all her savings had been spent. Since she couldn't pay her rent, she couldn't face her landlord. Her credit card and other bills were piling up and she needed to put food on the table.

This caused her to suffer from panic attacks and anxiety. Anxiety turned into hopelessness…which turned into depression.

She was on the edge and planned to end her life through drug overdose.

While kneeling and crying out in despair to God, a sudden feeling of trepidation was placed in her mind. Her heart was racing like something dark was about to happen.

It was the fear of the afterlife and fear for the future of her kids that made her pause. Meanwhile, while she was gripped by this fear that came upon her so suddenly, her phone was beeping – as messages of hope poured in.

Patsy, her godly mentor (bless her heart), texted verse after verse of hope that reminded her of her hope in Jesus.

In hindsight, she couldn't help but give all praise to the God that redeems, the God that saw her lethargy, her loneliness and hopeless state.

At Patsy's gentle prompting, Marie underwent biblical deliverance to remove her from this oppressive state. There was light at the end of the tunnel!

Indeed God blesses His children with a spiritual family that lifts them up in difficult times and spurs them to move forward and live for God's purpose.

I, too, have been blessed by the promptings and help of a spiritual family. They have been actively praying and sending messages to impart strength to hold on to a life of faith.

Marie was able to rise above her thoughts of suicide with the help and support of God-given people and promptings of the Holy Spirit of God.

When things seemed to be going well for her family, Marie was confronted yet again with another heavy trial.

Her daughter Catherine (not her real name ) a twenty-two-year-old, fresh college graduate who was following her dream of becoming a nurse, was diagnosed with Stage 4 Lupus!

It was heart-wrenching for Catherine, to say the least because she was idealistic. She had big dreams of reaching her goal of becoming a nurse, one day. She was focused and persevered through college.

Marie was *crushed* like never before. Even in the worst of situations, she was able to rise above them, but *this* news she was confronted with, was too much for her to bear.

A dark, depressive mood hovered over their family as they had to endure this desolate path, while Catherine went through chemo and radiation treatments.

*This* massive amount of pain compelled Marie to totally surrender her life to the Lordship of Jesus Christ. He became Master of her life. She was freed from her past sins, freed from guilt and anger.

Layers upon layers of walls of despair and shame were broken down as she rested in the safety net of the Shepherd. Marie has been a great friend of mine for over ten years. Her friends helped her carry her burdens and have been with her on this journey.

Catherine was healed and a few years later, got married to a wonderful man!

In a span of ten years, her other daughter Jess (not her real name), at age 27, developed a lump in her breast and back pain. I can imagine Marie moaning and rolling her eyes and saying, "Another one, Lord?" It was like living through a never-ending nightmare!

They hopped from one doctor to another until a surgeon suggested a biopsy. Their worst fear became a reality. Jess had Stage 2 breast cancer!

Marie was grateful that God provided a solution, a surgical breast removal – which was done after two weeks. It was like her whole life was riddled with misfortunes, nonstop.

She came to a point of total surrender to the will of God through her despair. While on her knees she claimed the promises of God.

Indeed, she became a *relentless* woman. Coming out from this fiery furnace, she still managed to have a joyful and peaceful countenance.

While in despair, one must seek God and move one's focus from circumstances to the character of God. The book of Psalms is especially most comforting and encouraging when one is in agony. Psalm 34:18 says, *"The Lord is near to the brokenhearted and saves the crushed in spirit."*

When she waivers in her faith, she immediately recognizes her frailty, turns back to The Lord, and clings to His promises. Marie is grateful that she was taken out from darkness and brought to a joyful place where she is today. She experiences a peace that transcends all logic and worldly understanding.

Her daughters are recovering, and the Lord is supplying *all* their needs. Her past is a testament of God's **relentless** redeeming grace.

We may not fully understand His ways or why He allows suffering, but I know that it is always for a purpose. I know that His ways aren't our ways and His thoughts are far above ours yet Isaiah 59:1 says *"The Lord's hand that isn't short that it cannot save nor his ear dull to hear"*. Though He is seated on the throne above the earth, He is very near. But with our finite minds, we cannot fully comprehend His Supremacy, His transcendency and existence outside of space and time independent of anything or anyone.

Marie found the One Who gave her tranquility. She ran to the loving embrace of Jesus Christ. Her unfaltering attitude and steadfast endurance in the most difficult challenges come from a deep understanding of the heart of God.

I am deeply honored for this opportunity to write about Marie's life. I write from the outside, peering into the lives of these *relentless* men and women to whom I owe my deepest gratitude.

## Michael and Sandy – Through It All

I've had the privilege of presenting stories of people who have been radically transformed by a Relentless God.

The story of Michael and Sandy Uysiuseng is one of those I've had the pleasure of writing. Their life story is truly compelling and should be memorialized as a testament of Gods transforming power and grace.

They are wonderful, God-loving workers in the Lord's vineyard. I have nothing but admiration for Michael and Sandy's goodness, humility, and transparency. I thank them for allowing me to write their life story and share it in this book.

It is with great respect that I write this for the world to come to know the saving power of Jesus Christ.

The setting of this story was during the roaring 80s in the Philippines. Manila was the fashion capital of Asia then where the glitz and glamour was *unparalleled*. It was a time when the streets of Manila and Makati were filled with men and women, young and old, "dressed to the nines", ready to drink and party all night into the morning.

Nightclubs, discotheques, bars, and hotels were brimming with the most glamorous, wealthy, and most powerful people during that era. It was a memorable time such that to this day, the era is relived in stories told around the dinner table or at parties by those who survived those years.

I myself have vivid memories of those *"golden years"*. As I recall, it was also a time of an unbridled upswing of *decadence*.

Sandy and Michael were both from Cebu, a province in the Central part of the Philippines, known for its pristine beaches and historical landmarks from its 16th century Spanish colonial past. It is home to many of the Philippines wealthiest Spanish and Chinese families, including Michael's family.

Michael grew up in an extremely wealthy home that is intensely traditional and the practice of bowing to different gods was common in the religion he grew up in. Additionally, marrying someone from *outside* his Chinese ethnic background, was prohibited and shunned by family.

Despite this strict adherence to tradition, he became a rebellious child, having been ensnared by the wiles of the world.

This kind of lifestyle would cause most to self-destruct, create toxic behaviors that play with the subconscious. That's how it was for Michael.

Having read and listened to their testimonies, I was committed to knowing more because each of their life stories came with honest accounts that were powerful narratives that could help others.

Sandy's childhood memories were difficult for her to recount, without stirring overwhelming negative emotions. She was the eighth child from a large brood of eleven children, and she grew up in a very strict religious home.

Her intense and devout Catholic upbringing was overshadowed by a toxic family dynamic. She witnessed the drunkenness and violence of her father towards her siblings and her mother. It was a combination of poverty and the environment at home that led her to become a recluse.

The freedom to speak out about her emotions ebbed away, so she simply kept her thoughts and emotions to herself and developed an expertise of *being invisible* in their home.

In spite of everything, she developed a strong bond with her sisters and even lived with them throughout her college years. That's the environment Sandy grew up in, contending with an abusive father. Little did she know that her story would spiral into something even *more intense*.

In an attempt to allow Sandy to blossom and come out of her shell, her sisters prodded her to join beauty pageants, to which she obliged because she was attractive. She took to modeling jobs as well, and finally ended up working as a flight attendant.

Being a flight attendant during the 80s was a dream job because during those times, the experience of globe-trotting was only limited to the very wealthy.

For Sandy, this was a tremendous opportunity that she took seriously. It opened her world to a whole new adventure of traveling to places she had never dreamed of, in addition to learning the art of sophistication and glamour, which was a totally different lifestyle to the one she grew up in.

One thing was certain, that her once innocent life was now touched with worldly passions.

Michael trained under the tutelage of his father, who was the owner of the biggest undergarment manufacturer in the region. His father was razor-sharp when it came to business and was also very stern.

There was *much tension* between father and son. It was like "walking on eggshells" every time he was around his father. No mistake was overlooked, regardless of how trivial. Tensions as well as emotions quickly built up between father and son. And because of his rebellious ways, Michael's relationship with his demanding father was severely strained. Michael then decided to leave for Manila.

Sandy's completely disarming appeal, oozing with femininity with her unassuming, mysterious qualities were what captured Michael's heart. He was captivated by her.

In the same manner, Sandy was drawn to Michael, who had an air of ámour propre' about him. He was handsome, charismatic, well dressed and world-savvy. This appeal would be alluring to women especially those who were unacquainted with the ways of the world and grew up in sheltered environments.

That's how it was for Sandy. She fell for him right away and his persistence propelled her to take his advances seriously. Michael and Sandy's love story began.

They were drawn to each other like magnets and they romanced for a time.

Meanwhile, Michael's parents discovered their relationship and immediately disapproved of it. It was the combination of Sandy's poverty and ethnicity were the reasons she was rejected.

To be rejected because of one's ethnicity is totally demoralizing for the one on the receiving end. Angry and dejected by his parents' response toward their relationship, Michael had made it his resolve to purse their romance. After some time, he and Sandy decided to move in together and soon, a beautiful, bouncing baby girl was born.

Sandy moved up in her career resulting in more time *away* from Michael. The absence of Sandy allowed Michael more time to satiate himself with wild living. But even though he was well into his vices, he had an astute business sense. He had a remarkable ability to connect with people and had foresight when it came to business.

He was able to land a job that launched business prospects resulting in successful endeavors. However, pride quickly set in and his astounding arrogance hastened a life of leisure, earning him notoriety for philandering and being a party animal.

Michael's father who was committed to restore his relationship with his son, called him back to Cebu. Before accepting this tempting offer, Michael had a few conditions, one of which was marrying Sandy before leaving for Cebu. There was a glimmer of hope, or so Sandy thought.

She was overjoyed when Michael proposed to her despite his family's rejection of her. After her experience of being raised in a toxic environment, Sandy must have felt that she would finally experience the charmed life, an overwhelming happiness. I can picture her on cloud nine, practically floating on air, showing off her radiant smile as they wed in a simple but elegant ceremony in historic Manila.

Everything seemed to go well and it looked like their path was finally heading for a different direction. So Sandy resigned from her job and moved back to Cebu with her daughter Nikki in tow. They moved into a huge house with an enormous garden, an idyllic place that Sandy, Michael, and the children would enjoy immensely.

Taking over the reins of the family business was the ideal job for Michael, who was now the sole bread winner of a growing family.

As time passed, Michael was appointed General Manager of the company, giving him free reign to run the company the way that he saw fit. The father-son team became unified and their relationship was restored.

One would think that this was an ideal life. Who wouldn't be attracted to this life of luxury and comfort? Certainly, many of us would dream of this fairytale life and in fact, strive for this our whole lives. But this luxurious life that they were enjoying, proved to become a *nightmare* for Sandy.

One would think that Michael would come to his senses

and give up all his vices and take up his responsibilities as head of his growing family.

Life is made up of peaks and valleys; nobody ever expects that at the height of one's happiness, there would be a hard crash. Sandy never imagined that this dreamy, wistful life she had been enjoying, would turn her world upside down into a wretchedly mournful existence.

Sandy recalls the nights or early mornings when Michael would come home to her with a string of hickeys on his neck and scratch marks on his back, coming from a night of booze and indulging in immoral acts with women. At this point they already had three children.

This nightmare continued for fifteen long grueling years and yet Sandy still hung on to the toxic, destructive relationship. Someone once said that "the scars you can't see, are the ones hardest to heal".

In spite of Michael's behavior, Sandy never attempted to follow him to a bar nor read his phone messages, but hung on to hope and trusted that things would get better. She didn't realize that the scars deep inside her heart were beginning to take root with a feeling of numbness. Coping with the pain from the unfaithfulness and disloyalty of a spouse is different for every person.

Some hurt themselves violently. Others hurt the cheating spouse and leave. Some others file for divorce right away. And yet others choose to suffer in silence, look the other way, and become numb.

Betrayal has devastating effects and it is oftentimes difficult to manage one's emotions. There is shock, agitation, fear, pain and most often *depression*. During this dark night of her soul, Sandy decided to look the other way and resigned herself to her fate by being engrossed in domestic duties, caring for the kids, and the home. During times of rest, she would pick up a book which provided great therapy for her aching heart.

It was Christmas eve, the year 1996, when Michael received the most devastating news. His father whom he had come to respect and love, was brutality murdered while driving his car!

This shook his world and his resolve. His life was about to be totally shattered. Soon after, his mom who had been estranged from her husband, took control and ownership of the family business, a business that Michael was trained to run one day.

Because of the dysfunctional relationship he and his mom had, he ended up selling all his shares of the company. He and Sandy used the money from the sale to venture into another business. As if it weren't bad enough that he continued to indulge himself with his many vices, their business partner betrayed them, resulting in a failed business venture!

Embittered and totally dispirited, Sandy reached a point of exasperation. They were no longer able to supply the needs of their family. Their savings were depleted, having only several hundred pesos in their account which wasn't enough to feed their growing brood.

They moved from the mansion they got so comfortable living in, to a tiny apartment as their savings were almost totally consumed.

It reached a point when they even had to pull their children *out of school* and sought ways to feed their growing family. Sandy was distraught and desperate, not only because of their bleak misfortune, but Michael resorted to experimenting with dangerous drugs which made him spiral into addiction! They hit rock bottom…and any sense of security and hope that was left, was completely shredded.

While Michael's response to stress was to turn to drugs, Sandy's was being driven to seek the Lord.

They were oblivious to the fact that this dismal place they were in, was going to be used by the Almighty God to knock on the doors of their hearts and change their circumstances.

Sometimes God allows us to go through desert experiences to shatter our stubborn self-will, causing us to look up and see that there is a shelter to run to. In Jesus there is *always* hope.

By God's **relentless** mercy, He heard the prayers of a *relentless soul*. Sandy was brokenhearted and cried out to God, and He heeded the plea of a devastated yet tender-hearted woman who decided to stay in the relationship while crying out to God. She acknowledged that the religious rituals she was accustomed to growing up, never gave her real peace, especially now that she'd reached the lowest point of her life.

While in this desperate state, a neighbor reached out to her and invited her to attend a Sunday service. She accepted.

It was at that particular moment and that specific place where God's Word from Matthew 11:28-30 was read. *"Come to me all you who are weary and burdened, and I will give you rest"*, resonated deep within her despairing heart. Then more comforting words flowed *"Take my yoke upon you and learn from Me, for I am gentle and humble in heart and you will find rest for your souls"*. A flood of tears *burst forth* from her eyes! She realized that this special time was God's way of lifting her burdens from her. Indeed, God was answering her prayers!

It wasn't long before she surrendered her life to the Lordship of Jesus, which to Sandy, was a breath of fresh air that she was in dire need of!

She immersed herself in God's Word and decided to join an all-women's discipleship group. These women carried her burdens with her, and painstakingly prayed for her husband Michael.

Before she came to faith with this wonderful Savior, her heart had become numb towards her husband as perhaps as defense mechanism of the mind. Nothing remained to bind their relationship any longer.

But GOD!

God, in all His mercy and compassion, patience and power, restored their love for one another. There was honesty, an admittance and recognition of failures and faults as Michael confessed his sins to God and his spouse.

Michael, broken and humbled through the circumstances of his life, soon decided to follow Jesus, too! They both acknowledged that no amount of wealth could ever give them real joy. It's only Jesus. God can break through and soften the soils of the hardest of hearts and bring one to true faith and love for Him.

The *relentless* mercy of a Relentless God searches out the lost ever so faithfully and gives hope to the parched heart, showing mercy to those who are desperate and those who earnestly seek Him. He gives peace to the restless and forgives the sins of His beloved creation who have put their faith in His Son Jesus.

The story of Sandy and Michael touched by God in such a powerful a way, reflects the love story of the Lord Jesus Christ with humanity.

One would think that it was impossible for someone who was imprisoned by sin that so easily entangles, could ever be transformed into a gentle, humble servant of Christ. Who would have thought that Michael and Sandy's once destructive relationship would culminate into an affectionate, beautiful love each passing day?

Who would've thought that Michael would end up accepting Sandy's invitation to worship service and surrendering his life to Jesus? The transforming power of the Holy Spirit was evident in Michael's life, as well as Sandy's. Michael immediately quit all his vices, including his addiction to porn, drugs and even cigarettes, and was physically, emotionally, mentally restored!

They both now lead and help other couples to know The Lord. They are actively involved in the different ministries of the church including being part of church leadership!

I am so privileged to know these humble and godly harvesters for God's kingdom. In fact, their daughter Nikki is married to my son Silas. They decided to walk that path of righteousness as well.

As I marvel at the love story of this great pair whom God restored, I am awestruck with wonder at the love, forgiveness, and restoration of Our Amazing God.

## Relentless Survivor

It is an honor to write the life story of a close friend of mine whom I have known for over 15 years. It is with great humility that I present this inspirational piece that captivates and is vital in learning lessons about the consequences of the choices we make.

Her story is a very familiar one. It takes me back to the major motion picture way back in the 90s entitled *"Not Without My Daughter"* starring Sally Field. It was controversial for its ethnic undertones but still well received by some for its theme about a helpless woman in danger and would've been interesting to have it as a case study on ethnic cultures.

Yet, here was my friend, who had a very similar narrative (in a different country), with the same familiar emotions as she related her life story to me.

Genevieve Nandi, "Ginni" for short, was the woman in danger, in a place not her home, in a culture totally divergent from what was normal to her.

She was once married to Zachary (not his real name), a man with a gentle spirit and an open heart. He wasn't of the same faith but willing to listen to the gospel. He was handsome with dark locks and dark expressive eyes to match. He was faithful to her as he was courteous and unassuming to us.

Nobody would ever suspect that the series of events that were about to take place would be a dramatic unfolding of a *perilous* journey and an unforeseen *bleak* future.

This poignant story started when the family moved from the Philippines, to her husband's country, with two of their precious jewels (a daughter and a son) in tow.

Her beautiful seven year old daughter had dark, expressive eyes and at such a young age, one could determine what she was thinking just by looking at her gaze. Her son Joshua was the cutest baby boy with dark locks just like his father's. Both of them had an innocent, luminous glow of happiness by simply being with their parents.

Ginni and her children had no clue what was in store for them nor was she aware of a gloomy dark cloud that hovered over them.

They were ushered into her husband's parent-owned building of 6 floors. It was the top floor that they made their dwelling which was already set up for them, including a dental clinic for her husband.

She hadn't realized how wealthy they were since Zachary was so simple in the way he dressed and embraced the simplicity of their lifestyle. The ground floor was the family-owned meat shop. Her mother in-law's residence on the fourth floor was enormous with three or four salons.

The floor she was ushered into was ornate, designed with gold leaf and crystals. Windows were high and adorned with thick drapes similar to a palace of a royal household. She was spellbound and caught herself agape, staring, stunned in disbelief.

There were two dining areas. Each one showcased a dining table that could seat nineteen people! From bedrooms to salons to dining areas to the cutlery – all had the same elegant flair.

The kitchen was expansive and contained three massive freezers. This kind of household could mean that they had a huge family with enormous appetites, *or* they liked to entertain powerful, wealthy guests, or *both*.

The ground floor was the family-owned meat shop.

Some women would easily renounce any ties they had with their past to live in this kind of environment where they could have anything they wished for.

Of course, some things come at a heavy price. Sometimes it costs them something that they hold so dear. Would they be willing to give up their life? Their faith? It is with trials like this that tests one's faith. How fast does one hold on to one's life and liberty?

Zachary's family lived in a certain place in the country that upheld the traditions of their fathers. In fact, it was located in the most conservative and most traditional part of that country.

Ginni suffered from extreme culture shock; she felt like she was losing her identity. Living in a foreign land, there was extreme mental pressure to comply with what was normal to the locals.

Since the family would entertain guests nearly every night, she would be doing her familial duties of washing dishes until midnight and was prohibited from making lengthy phone calls to her family in Manila.

She was in dire need of respite and connection with a spiritual family and longed to worship the way she knew how. She found a Baptist International church which she frequented with Zachary. This gave her a sense of belonging with familiar ties to her faith that she held tightly to.

The missionaries whom she was so close to, sent her messages from the scriptures to encourage here during those impossible times. Prayers for Ginni was a part of our Sunday worship.

Zach no longer followed in the traditional way of his fathers and they were going to town every week to worship at the church. Zach's family quickly came to the conclusion that they were doing things behind their backs, wandering from the faith of their fathers.

Ginni was considered a bad influence on her husband. They blamed her for taking him away from their faith, enticing him to follow 'the way of Cain'.

One day, when they arrived back home, they found their bedroom ransacked. His brothers discovered her bible wrapped in newspaper, along with some gospel tracts. They were likely extremely angry but kept their silence. In the meantime, they contrived a plan to pull Zach and Ginni apart.

As a result of their plan, Zachary was torn between his wife and his mother. He made a decision to move out to avoid further confrontations and to keep the peace.

At first, the family didn't agree with their move but on the persistence of Ginni, they finally agreed, to give them more time to plan.

After this, a series of events took place that rendered Ginni totally desperate.

It was an uphill battle that needed perseverance and determination and uncompromising faith. To fight a battle such as this, one had to come to terms with reality and learn to trust that the powerful God that was preached, the same God of Abraham, Isaac, Jacob, David, Paul and John, was and is the same faithful, powerful God that would bring His children through a tough situation.

It wasn't only going to be tough, but a seemingly hopeless one.

The dark cloud that hovered over their new home turned into a hurricane! Ginni came home one day to an empty house. Her children and her husband were all gone!

She was baffled! She went to check their closets. They were wiped clean. Not a single piece of clothing was left! She was in the state of shock, stuck in the moment, grappling with the reality that her family had been taken from her!

She clung on to her chest while her heartbeat was racing, beating out of control and she was blanketed in the intense emotions of fear, anxiety, and pain.

As her heart felt shredded from within her, a hysterical cry overcame her!

When she recounted these events, I was completely dumbfounded. I couldn't imagine going through this myself. It's unthinkable.

In her exhaustion from crying hysterically and thinking of worst-case scenarios, she eventually fell asleep.

There is a defense mechanism that a lot of us go through in times of extreme emotional and mental anguish. The brain puts us in a "suspended time capsule".

Whenever Ginni had to cope with this dire situation, she'd curl up in a fetal position, and sleep, thus, escaping reality.

When she awoke, questions raced through her head, "How will I get back my children with very little money?"

She had no work, neither did she know anyone influential. How indeed was she going cope? Her desperation to get her children back drove her to totally surrender to God.

Yes, they may be wealthy and perhaps even influential, but not one of them could be greater than God, The Most powerful El Shaddai, who created the vastness of the universe and the earth and everything in it! She knew He would make a solution to this hopeless situation.

It was now between her and God. She didn't know the plans of God, but she knew that she needed to trust in His plan, His timing, and His ways.

She went to her husband's clinic with questions and a desperate plea. Zach didn't want his wife to make a scene there in the clinic, assuaged her fears and told her that she could go to their family house to see her beloved children. He even gave her money for a taxi.

Upon reaching the posh house of her in-laws, she was ushered in and seated in one of the elegant salons. Her mother in-law was caught between her faith and her love of her son.

A mother meddling in the marriage and family life of a son was unheard of where Ginni was from.

She informed Ginni that they were already divorced, and was asked to sign the papers to be processed in court!

Ginni was so shocked, a flood of tears burst from her eyes. "Was this real? How could this be happening?!"

Questions flooded her mind. It seemed like her faculties were not working properly since she felt sudden chills on her arms, and her legs were unable to move. She wasn't ready to face the gravity of the situation.

Then came the worst news. They asked her to renounce her faith in Jesus, or face not ever seeing her children again! After coming face to face with the news about the divorce which struck her like a thunderbolt, she thought that she was going to feel weaker or helpless with this even more horrifying news.

The opposite happened.

During this time, when she had reached the crossroads of her life, she felt the strength and inner promptings of the Holy Spirit within her coming to the surface.

She said that she was ready to die for her faith. She would never give up her precious Jesus. Zach's brothers started coming out one by one, trying to convince her to give up her Jesus. And she gave a firm answer "No!"

One brother said, "Your brain is going to kill you". They couldn't understand her stubborn faith. I guess they weren't prepared for her resolve of not giving up her God. She gave another firm answer, "*I can never give up Jesus. I am ready to die.*"

Our true condition before God is exposed in the toughest of circumstances. There are some that give up their faith so easily with just small problems. There are those who appear strong in faith at first, then crumble when the going gets tough. Yet there are some who, when the rubber meets the road, remain steadfast under enormous amounts of pressure.

As God told Joshua in Joshua 1:9 *"Have I not commanded you? Be strong and courageous! Do not tremble or be dismayed, for the Lord your God is with you wherever you go."* God repeats this command in other verses in the book of Deuteronomy and other verses in Joshua.

Ginni was given *supernatural* strength and insight. She was uncompromising and courageous despite being surrounded by the entire family. She was asked to leave and call when she wanted to visit, while they continued the process of divorce.

Her next step of going to the consulate was a letdown because they told her to take the easier road – which was to give up her faith and convert.

Had they no other advice than that? They likely knew she wasn't going to go along with it, so they offered help instead by telling her that they would be willing to "pass the hat" on her behalf.

After a while, they helped her by giving her someone to translate what was written in the documents for divorce.

During those moments Ginni actually needed the moral support from a countryman, while she went back to face those in the consulate. The translator gave her a warning that there were other women with similar cases, and they completely lost any connection their kids because the family had taken them to another country. Surely, this was inconceivable! It's an immoral act to separate one's children from their mother.

She returned a second time to the posh house of her in-laws which she concluded was an epic failure because they refused to give her the children unless she gave up her Jesus. She stood her ground and said that she would not give up the very One who had given her hope that was even more precious than anything or anyone, even her children!

If she signed the divorce papers, she would be free, but they'd have authority to take her daughter Andrea since she was of age; but her son Joshua was still nursing, so by law they would have to give him back to her.

But they, too, were adamant. They told her that they would take *both* her children.

Her in-laws prohibited her from getting in touch with her children. She tried calling daily, but someone would yank the phone out of her daughter's hand, or they would answer and simply give some flimsy excuse.

She went back to their residence, alone this time, her resolve unbending. Upon seeing her mother in-law, she hugged her, and she appealed to her motherly instinct. Ginni bent down, groveled, kissed her feet over and over and begged her to let the children go. She was surrounded by ten people expecting her to sign the papers.

There was a moment of serendipity. What if she agreed momentarily to sign the documents? Would they ease up?

Would they be kinder to her? She did agree to sign the papers, but only for that moment. She then asked to be allowed to see her husband *before* signing the papers. They agreed but disallowed eye contact with him and speaking in the vernacular (Filipino) which Zachary was fluent in.

Zach appeared in the salon looking forlorn. Ginni was surprised to see how old he looked. His once dark curly locks were now sprayed with greys, and his smooth skin was now wrinkled. He looked like he'd aged by at least ten years!

She bowed her head as she spoke, though she thought it wise to speak to him in a language that only both of them understood. Defying her in-laws, she looked up at him and gazed into his eyes as she spoke to him, paying no attention to the efforts her in-laws made in trying to muzzle her. She begged him to let the children go. She warned him too, that she was willing to die and her blood would be splattered all over the floor that day! Zach was so shocked at her words that he raised his voice at his family and cried, ***"Let them go! Give her the children!"***

Suddenly there was a sound of death that the women around them made, a sound of mourning that resonated all throughout the building and the next.

Ginni bolted to the kitchen to grab a garbage bag and rushed for the children's room to dump all their things in. Upon seeing her, the kids ran to her and hugged her. They wailed!

In their innocent minds, they hadn't been aware of what had just happened nor did they have any idea why their mom had been taken away from them.

I assume that the wailing from Andrea and Joshua were a mixture of fear and an intense feeling of relief of being rescued by their beloved mom.

As soon as they left the building, *miraculously*, there was a taxi on the other side of the road! Normally, taxis were scarce and took a while to get one. But this time, the taxi was ready and available.

Due to the loud cries of mourning from women in the neighborhood as Ginni and her children were leaving, the police *could've* been there at any moment, they *could* have her imprisoned and *could've* returned the children to her in-laws. But *this* didn't happen. There was *supernatural* intervention!

The taxi driver asked their destination. She didn't have a clue where to go but asked to be brought away from that area. She didn't have money nor did she have a roof over their heads. The taxi driver told them that he knew a Filipino woman who could help her. You see, when God takes care of his own, He does it with so much passion. He changed situations and circumstances which changed the course of history of mother and children.

The taxi driver brought her to the Filipino woman who was married to a local. They welcomed them into the restaurant and into their home. They fed them and treated them with compassion and understanding. The Italian restaurant was elegant, fit for private gatherings for the wealthy. The Filipino woman, who was in good standing with the manager of the restaurant, allowed Ginni and her daughter Andrea to help out, and allowed Joshua to hang around as they did their jobs.

With all the events from the past weeks, Ginni felt numb, while confusion and fear overtook her. Fear of the possibility that she could be arrested, and the children could be returned to the family of their father.

She had no other choice but to try and find a way for the children go back to the Philippines, safe in the arms of Ginni's family. But it was like trying to look for a needle in a haystack. How would she be able to do this? How would she find someone to help her through this mess?

As these were going through her mind, there came an answer for the deepest cry of her heart. A certain gentleman came to her rescue and was an answer to her prayers, not for favors of any other kind, but to simply help her out. The gentleman had seen her hanging clothes in the garden of a neighbor and asked the host family if he could invite her to the barbecue.

Ginni was hesitant but since it was just a barbecue, she didn't find anything wrong with it. It was nearly Christmas and it was a time for celebration among the community of expatriates and she, together with Andrea and Joshua, were invited to dinner at a fancy hotel. It was at this dinner where she was interviewed by the gentleman regarding the events of her life.

She poured out her heart and related the events that transpired from the time she set foot in that country to that moment. One could come to the conclusion that it was her transparency, authenticity and the poignant storytelling which moved him to help her.

But the truth is that God did that.

The gentleman offered to buy plane tickets for the children. They could finally be set free from any form of repercussions!

Ginni, on the other hand, would have to save up for her own plane fare, so she continued working in the restaurant.

There was a dilemma, however. When the time came for them to leave, they were stopped by Immigration. By law, children were prohibited to travel without a parent or a guardian. Ginni was separated from them to be interviewed by immigration officers. The throbbing of her heart became intense as they took her to a room to be interrogated. She was gripped with fear.

Anything could happen. She could lose her precious kids, be imprisoned, or punished severely! She asked God to give her *another miracle* and kept praying until the tide turned. She was told that the kids could leave *only* with the consent of the father.

Things were getting really perilous and she needed God to come through for them. She needed His divine strength to go through this valley she was in, at that moment.

The officers picked up the phone and dialed her husband's hand phone, clinic phone, and home phone. Miraculously, all three lines were busy!

Her prayers and all who prayed with her, were answered! If anyone in the family or her husband answered the phone, it would've been a different scenario altogether. She would've faced incarceration and the kids would've been sent back to their father.

However, since the officers couldn't connect with Zach, her children were *not* permitted to fly out of the country.

The airline crew was very sympathetic to them. They probably sensed her despair, or she may have likely given out distress signals. The crew told her that they would contact her when they could find someone to escort and act as the children's guardian.

That was so brave of them to help her! It was another needle in a haystack. She needed another intervention from God. *"Another one Lord. Another one please,"* was her plea.

The airline crew called one day and said that there was a Filipino couple who was willing to help them since they were going back to the Philippines for a break. They worked with a Royal family and therefore things would be made possible, since they didn't need to pass the immigration officers for interrogation, nor the airport police! It was a quick and uneventful handover. She tried to keep her composure as her kids looked back and stared at her with sadness written in their faces. It was heart-wrenching for her, but she didn't have any choice. She had to hold back her tears so there wouldn't be any suspicion that would trigger any intervention from the police.

Ginni was *not* permitted to inform her family in Manila until the children were about to land to avoid being intercepted by authorities.

As she recalled the events, she was deep in thought – as if reliving that very moment. She didn't know whether anyone would be able to pick them up on such short notice or if anyone would pick up the call at all!

But God was in full control of everything. The family of Ginni came through for the children! They were relieved to see that the kids arrived without a hitch.

While I was listening to the events unfolding, I had become aware of the reality of the faithfulness, mercy, compassion of our *relentless* God.

There was miracle after miracle. Impossibilities became possible.

This is the story about the God who never leaves His children to fend for themselves alone. As the story moved along, we see the hand of God, making things happen, giving Ginni wisdom and discernment, creating and changing affairs, hearts, and pathways.

Ginni is now back in her beloved homeland – the Philippines, serving the Lord and enjoying every minute of it.

She abandoned her "life in the past", living in the foreign country, yet without forgetting the work of a powerful God that held her closely and changed entire situations to rescue this helpless woman in peril.

She is a relentless survivor and through the years, she had established a successful business that offers an early reading program to young kids as early as three years old.

When she looked back at this particular story of her life, she marveled at how quickly the events of her life unfolded. She has now remarried to a wonderful godly man who totally relates to her in a loving, respectful way. And she's enjoying the serenity after the storm.

Ginni was *moved to tears*, and I was, too – while she narrated her story to me.

This compelling true to life story should be made into a movie because it will leave the audience completely spellbound.

## Finally Home

It was March 2020. The hospitals were overwhelmed with COVID-19 patients as the outbreak was gaining momentum in Manila, Philippines. It hadn't reached its peak then, but the cases were increasing daily.

Medical practitioners were called to put in extra time because the health system was crashing. The Philippines was totally unprepared for this kind of pandemic, which overtook the world.

In the midst of this crisis, my daughter-in law Nikki became ill with Steven Johnson Syndrome, a grave allergic reaction that nearly cost her life!

She was in dire need of help at the moment – and my son Silas, for fear of his wife catching the dreaded COVID-19 on top of her illness, opted to stay put in their home. With our persistence and with the help of my friends, they had no choice but to go and join the long line of patients amid the infection.

It was a stressful time for *all* of us and we were petrified because she needed medical attention right away…and the long wait *could* cause her to perish!

My husband and I were abroad then, and we felt helpless. We contacted people to pray for them and doctors to help out.

Nikki's parents who lived outside of Manila, were praying alongside us. Like us, they were in constant communication with Nikki and Silas.

It was during this time, that I met an amazing woman – Gina Rodriguez.

As I relived those horrifying moments, crying out to God the entire night, I was glad that I had the confidence at that time to ask for prayers for them.

Gina Rodriguez answered my texts right away. They were so calming and assured me that she and her husband Pastor Albit, were there for us. They prayed with us and oftentimes checked up on them.

Gina and Albit Rodriguez are the Bible teachers and spiritual parents of my son Silas and his wife Nikki.

It is her story that I wish to write because even in those brief times of correspondence through texts, she gave me great encouragement, and I had a glimpse of the woman that she was and is.

She stayed on and continued texting me, even after that incident. She helped me pray for the success of a book I was writing, and for a friend of mine who was dying of cancer.

What an irony that was. She was praying for my sick friend while she herself was in need of fervent prayers. I enjoyed our correspondences as we interceded for one another.

Even during those times that she was interceding in prayers for others, I had no clue about her cancer journey prior to this nor did I know that she was in pain then.

I will never forget her selfless act and her words that I've treasured in my heart. I discovered that she had a persistent pain *only* when she asked for prayers for her PET CT scan.

Then the correspondence stopped.

I found out the horrifying results from her daughter Bianca. She was in the advanced stage of cancer that metastasized to her liver, lungs, and other soft tissues.

This took me completely by surprise. I would've never imagined that she had cancer, much less an aggressive kind!

Bianca, her youngest daughter, and Gina's look-a-like, was part of our bible study group in Singapore. I was overjoyed to meet her and know that she's the daughter of my newfound friend Gina.

I usually checked up on Gina through Bianca and it was through Bianca that I gathered the life story of her mom. It was with great honor and esteem that I now write this chapter on Gina's life. I was given this wonderful privilege to write her journey and I'm grateful to her family for allowing me to do so.

Gina was a beautiful, tender hearted, godly woman who made it her life goal to glorify God in all circumstances and all her life.

Her husband Albit and Gina opened their home to many couples. They met with several groups in their home – to disciple them and bring them to the knowledge of Jesus Christ.

My son Silas and Nikki attest to the the truth of Albit and Gina's hospitality and godly character. They are great stewards of truth which spurred Silas and Nikki to dive deeper into the Scriptures and even desiring to be enrolled in a bible academy.

After discipling many groups, Albit was asked to be a lay pastor and an elder at Christ Commission Fellowship, a difficult but necessary ministry that oversees the affairs of the mega-church.

Meanwhile, Gina actively served the Lord and was a founder of a ministry devoted to women, teaching them, counseling them, and bringing them to knowledge of our Lord.

In 2014, Women2women ministry was born wherein she and her daughters served.

Bianca shared more insight into the ministries and passion of her mom. I'm sure that few knew about her talent in interior design, which she put to good use with her own resources.

Gina's elegance was showcased in her clothing line, Tango, where I used to shop because they had very affordable prices. She made every event in the church beautiful, just like their home, and just like her. I am sure that she made everything beautiful, not only with her talent but she graced every event with her kindness and tenderness.

I am inspired by her testimony. I heard stories of how excited she was about seeing the Lord during her last days. She would wake up from her sleep and ask, "Oh, am I still here?" She looked forward to being with her Lord Jesus and excited to see heaven.

Bianca updated me on events of her mom's last days.

Because of the rising number of cases in Manila, her dad and mom advised Bianca not to come home at such a time. Her mom begged her to stay safe in Singapore where she lived with her husband Marti.

But being so far away from her beloved mom who was on the brink of dying, Bianca knew that she had to be home to spend the remaining days with her mom. In spite of the persistence of her mom on wanting to keep her daughter safe, Bianca flew back to the Philippines. She spent those memorable remaining days with her mom.

I am relating her cancer journey through both her husband Pastor Albit's account and her daughter's. I'm grateful to him for sharing his testimony and allowing me to write her story. I'm humbled and blessed to have this great opportunity to honor a fellow servant whom I admire and who served as a great impact to many women, including myself.

It started in 2019 when Gina felt pain in her abdominal and pelvic area. They sought various specialists who couldn't find a proper diagnosis. Everyone was baffled because there wasn't cancer detected nor other critical markers that were determined.

It was a few months after, while attending a major event of the church in Singapore, that the pain intensified and became *excruciating*.

Back in Manila, Gina still experienced a nagging pain. She was given a bleak diagnosis. It was called Squamous Cell Carcinoma, Cancer stage 3b that was causing the pain!

The next three months were spent on chemo and radiation treatments resulting in malaise with *terrible* side effects.

The side effects of cancer have a debilitating effect on the body. I've witnessed people lose pounds upon pounds of weight and couldn't even ingest food or medication without throwing up. I've witnessed people cry and beg God to remove the pain. The suffering of one who is stricken with this deadly disease extends to the family and to all those who surround them.

After the chemo-radiation treatment sessions, the Rodriguez's family received good news. December 2019 was a cause for celebration. They received the news that the tumor had disappeared, and they were no traces of cancer cells remaining in her body!

Everyone was jubilant and thankful that they could look forward to spending time with their precious mom and wife.

Gina soon began her period of convalescence. They were able to celebrate her 60th birthday in February 2020 with a feeling of grateful bliss and blessed by the favor that God had granted them.

Soon after the merriment, their hopes of her being completely healed, hit rock bottom.

She experienced pain in her lower abdomen and hip once more. It was that time in March when they were supposed to go for another PET CT scan to determine the underlying cause of her pain.

But since the hospitals were overwhelmed with COVID patients, she opted to postpone the procedure.

By April, she began to complain about the pain in various parts of her body. Her family thought that it could be bone-related arthritis or something similar.

What they discovered next became their *worst* nightmare. The cancer had metastasized to her liver, lungs, bones, spleen, scalp, and eye. This was a most devastating time for any family since they would be facing difficult times ahead.

Albit was always by his wife's side but because he knew his purpose in life, he still managed to lead online bible studies despite the pain of witnessing his wife suffer.

As the cancer aggressively spread throughout her body, they spent enormous amounts of time in deep prayer and much reflection.

It is difficult to grasp the enormity of their pain. It's even *more* difficult to accept that a beloved spouse who has been with you for over thirty or forty years was bearing the brunt of the pain, braving the agony.

I can't imagine seeing one's beloved, one's partner in ministry, whose prayers and devotion created such an impact in your wellbeing and in your transformation, deteriorate each day.

How does one cope during these bleak, dark times? How does one stay faithful in the Lord? How does one heal? How does one accept that one's wife could leave soon?

They were forced to face the hard facts that the Lord could very well be calling her home, as another PET scan confirmed their greatest fears. Through the darkest of times, nobody can discount the fact that the grace of God was evident.

The voice clip that Bianca sent me was surprising. It didn't sound like a woman dying or in pain! It was a voice of a woman who had so much wisdom to share with corresponding energy and enthusiasm.

Gina encouraged her loved ones around her to look at the goodness of the Lord in the valley of life. She quoted from Psalm 34:19 that read: *"The righteous person may have many troubles, but the Lord delivers him from them all."* She clearly saw that for every problem she had, God sent a solution.

She talked about having to go through the valley because it is through the valleys that we experience the nearness of the Shepherd. She had wisdom even in dying. She wasn't wallowing in self-pity nor was she dreading the inevitable.

The mercy and the nearness of the Shepherd was evident during those times of crisis. Gina's husband and the family scrambled to look for the much needed Morphine, a drug used to numb the pain of cancer patients.

God tapped the generous hearts of the church family to provide an overwhelming supply. Normally, one could get an ample supply from hospitals. But during the 2020 pandemic, morphine had become scarce because it was used as part of the treatment for COVID-19 patients.

God supplied all they needed through the generosity of their loved ones. They didn't have to raise funds or ask for help. In addition to this, their oncologist never charged them for his services!!

It is common for one going through the advanced stage of cancer, that there would be bone metastasis. That is when the bones become brittle and break, rendering more pain. One of the prayers that the family lifted up to the Lord was that Gina would not have to go through that.

God answered their prayers.

When we learn to see things from God's perspective, we **see His presence in our circumstances** no matter how dark the days are. Gina had learned that principle, and during her darkest moments, she saw the helping hand of God. She recognized His divine nature of love and mercy – that's why in the midst of her grave illness, she was able to counsel and encourage some women.

I am writing this, deep in thought, mixed with melancholy and joy. As I read Pastor Albit's and Bianca's accounts, I can't help but be awed by such a beautiful response to adversity.

I've captured what Albit wrote in his testimony about his loving wife. "*As her sickness rapidly ravaged her body, spreading to each and every part of her body rendering her partially blind, and her energy began to decline, she spent her last few days, giving advice to us (her family) on how to continue with God's work.*"

I was just so humbled at how one could still be preoccupied with others, with her family's spiritual lives – even in the midst of her weakness, double vision, nausea, and pain.

August 12, 2020 was the day Gina went home to be with the Lord.

Her life ended on earth, but she is now enjoying her eternal inheritance and worshipping her King and Master – the Lord Jesus Christ.

I haven't heard a more endearing story of one about to meet her Savior and I could only hope that when that day comes and I am about to leave, that I would have the same mindset and attitude, excited to see My Lord and leaving a godly legacy to the ones who come after me.

As the Psalmist says in Psalm 116:16 *"Precious in the sight of The Lord is the death of His faithful servants"* so is the death of Gina Rodriguez whose legacy lives on in the hearts of her family and those whom she touched.

Her name will be remembered in the church, in small groups, in this book as a memorial to a good and faithful servant of God.

I would like to share the lyrics of a song that inspired me help a friend of mine to face the inevitable. Gina Rodriguez was praying alongside me for that friend – Therese Necio-Ortega, who asked me to help her go through death and live her remaining days with joy in Christ.

I asked Therese's care giver to play this song daily to give her comfort so that she would look forward to seeing Jesus.

The melody is as beautiful as the song. I would like to thank Carolyn Tanchi-Pedro for this song which captures the profound truth behind life after death for the believer.

This song reminds me of the enduring faith of Gina and her heart's desire to see Jesus. I imagined her being welcomed in paradise amongst the heavenly hosts and especially Jesus who stretches out His arms in loving embrace and tells her *"You are now well and safe. Welcome, my faithful servant, well done."*

This beautiful song that Carolyn composed gives so much comfort and peace to those who have anchored their faith in Jesus Christ. May the cancer journey of Gina and the lyrics of this song resonate in the hearts of people and move them to find comfort and peace.

## Finally Home
By Dr. Carolyn Tanchi-Pedro

"I close my eyes and wake up to eternity.
I see the light of the face of Jesus Christ
I hear His voice calling out my name, Saying well done!
My good and faithful child
You're finally home. No more crying fear or pain,
No more darkness sin or shame.
I'm finally home where I belong, In the presence of My King.
I am finally home, bowed at His throne,
Worshipping his Majesty,
There's no place I'd rather be,
Full of love and hope and peace
No eye has seen, no eye has heard
What God has in store for those who love Him, joy abounds,
Streets of gold, springs of life, a light
the shines forth for His Glory.

It's everlasting.
No more crying fear or pain, No more darkness sin or shame
I'm Finally home, where I belong
In the presence of my King,
I'm finally home, bowed at His throne,
Worshipping His majesty
There's no place I'd rather be, full of love and hope and peace,
And I know, those of earth,
might feel the sting of death in all the place that I've left
But they must know, it's not the end,
There's a better place, prepared of them.
In Christ we'll meet again
I'm finally home, where I belong, In the presence of My King
I'm finally home singing His song for all eternity…"

Here's the YouTube video link if you'd like to listen to the song: https://youtu.be/R7jUTr71ITw

    I pray for the healing of the entire family of Gina and Albit Rodriguez. May the memory of your wife and Mom whom you hold so dear and close to your hearts, bring you the sweetness of God's loving embrace.

    I leave with you this verse from Numbers 6:24-26 "The Lord bless you and keep you; The Lord make His face shine upon you and be gracious to you; The Lord turn his face toward you and give you peace."

## In Pursuit of the Upward Call

When I think about the persecution of the Christian church, I feel an overwhelming sense of oneness with them. I feel pain, mixed in with great admiration.

As I sat through the film "Tortured for Christ", I felt an overpowering feeling of respect.

One can't help but wonder how they could hold on to their faith so strongly in spite of being placed under tremendous constant pressure, flagellation, insults, physical, emotional and verbal abuse.

And so with the disciples who followed Jesus. History has proven that they, too, suffered tremendously, and their death was catastrophic – yet they were willing to undergo such torture.

I read a lot of comments about the movie "The Passion of Christ". There are those that labeled it too graphic and named it the most violent film ever shown, instead of giving merit to its goal of portraying as closely as possible, what actually happened.

Instead of being moved by Christ's suffering, there were those who saw it as being outrageously violent. They failed to recognize that this was the most accurate picture of how Christ suffered and died for the sins of man.

While I agree it was violent, the fact is, we are confronted with the reality of His suffering. Without capturing that, it would water down the truth of what the Savior went through.

The movie was supposed to draw people to *the God who loves us* and Who sent His only Son to die for the sins of man.

There is a man from New Zealand who went to the Philippines to obey the call of God to share the good news of Jesus Christ. This is his story that I write.

Shane and his wife Rene are missionaries and dear friends of ours. I have great admiration for them because they have been relentlessly sharing the good news of Jesus Christ.

I'm entirely grateful for the sound teaching I received from the Christian Brethren missionaries. I've treasured them and taken the soundness of the Scriptures with me in my journey as I was called to teach the Word of God and mentor women.

Shane always taught us to persist in sound doctrine because this would give us a firm biblical foundation and an unwavering faith even if we go through the valleys of life.

Surprisingly, Shane started as an atheist for a number of years and reflected a life without God.

I've come across atheists before and it seems that their thoughts, lives and actions reflect the same pattern. I wonder sometimes, how they'd come to that conclusion: that there is no God.

How could they disregard the vastness of the universe and nature? When they looked up at the stars or looked around to see the beauty of creation, felt the calming breeze and heard the melodic sounds of the birds, didn't they ever stop to wonder how these came into existence?

Shane is a citizen of one of the most picturesque countries in the world.

New Zealand is known for the richness of its natural beauty with its snow-capped mountains and natural blue lakes. It has a perfect setting for God's creative backdrop with flowers in a myriad of colors, a wide variety of trees and shrubs that could easily evoke a smile and an inner gratitude to the One who bestowed such splendor to their country.

Creation is supposed to draw us to God, His attributes and divine nature.

In spite of being surrounded with such artistry, Shane was oblivious to his surroundings and lived for himself.

He didn't grow up in a happy home. Witnessing the violence of his dad toward his mom, caused him to become irate and easily outraged, even with the slightest provocation.

This got him in trouble at school a few times but it was also those outbursts of anger that made him excel in *contact sports* like rugby – which he really excelled at – wrestling, boxing and taekwondo.

Living only for the moment like Shane did, removes the worry about the past, present and future *until* you're confronted with a *catastrophic event*.

He was totally engrossed with gaining wealth, which he thought would bring him happiness – *until* his resolve was shaken.

It was nearing winter. It's the time of year when farmers roll the grass, stack them and cover them with polythene (aka polyethylene), allowing the grass to "cook" into a soft, brown and sweet food for the cows.

While he was rolling the silage stack, he hit an uneven patch of land, which caused the tractor to flip over backwards! As it steered backwards, his body wrapped around the steering wheel while it tumbled! It was a near fatal accident that disfigured his face.

He must have shattered his jawbone because the bottom half of his face had to be reconstructed. I would've never thought he'd been in an accident, much less a fatal one – because he now looks normal! They must have brilliant surgeons in New Zealand…there isn't even a trace of a bad fall!

He said he looked like Frankenstein for six weeks while he had smoothies and food that was blended and liquified. Nobody thought that he'd survive that accident because aside from him being wrapped in the steering wheel and under that heavy equipment, the tractor was "worth scrap"!

Aside from this near fatal accident, he also had a terrible accident in Rugby. Rugby is one of the toughest sports in the world. It's brutal and the nature of the game disallows the use of pads, helmets, or any protective gear, so it isn't any wonder that fatal accidents do occur.

At fifteen years old, he left school and took an apprenticeship with a local builder. He heard that the owner who was also his boss, was a born-again Christian and so were his co-workers.

So he prepared a speech for all to hear: *"I know you are Christians but I am an atheist. I don't want to be preached to about God. Good morning. I'm Shane."*

This introduction of himself came with a bold statement and a stern warning.

The guys respected his statement and didn't talk about God to him, but they did manage to "work around" this. Yes, Shane did make a bold statement, but the wise co-workers made a bolder step. They spoke about God *to* each other *within earshot of Shane!*

These wise fellows were persistent in sharing about God amongst themselves over the tough exterior of Shane. In his rebellion, he became more stubborn. His self-will and resolve were made of steel.

His accidents gave him a glimpse of the brevity of life. Indeed, some people are so arrogant and stubborn that they refuse to hear the "megaphone" of God, yet when confronted with death, they question if they were going to make it or face death. This happened to Shane. There was a chink in his atheistic armor of steel that cracked.

He was faced with a challenge from his co-worker one day. He confronted Shane with an unsettling question: *"You call yourself an atheist. So have you read the whole Bible to make that decision? Or was it based on what you were taught by others?"* One of the 'wise men' asked a thought-provoking question that would cause one to question even a seemingly immovable stance. He continued by making another equally bold statement: *"If you haven't read the Bible and yet made a decision to be an atheist, then you are a fool."*

Confronting someone who had previously warned everyone not to talk to him about God, is called ***courageous faith***. It takes supernatural courage to make such a statement especially to a stubborn man with an uncompromising stand. This courageous man was ready to face anything for the sake of the gospel.

When God stirs someone's heart to seek Him, soul searching becomes tantamount to searching for the truth. There are also stewards of truth who are obedient to the calling of God to share the gospel. That coworker of Shane, heeded God's call, and *that* divine appointment with him, is to be valued.

That started Shane's journey in search for the truth. He started having studies with a religious sect that didn't believe in the deity of Jesus Christ. This caused disputes and Shane's argument was valid.

He stated the fact that he was allowed to say "Jesus is not God" because Shane didn't believe in God, but he quipped *"You say you believe in God and then don't believe what He has written, why should I believe what you say then?"* It was logical reasoning.

The same thing happened with another religious sect who believed the same ideology. After these two sects couldn't answer his question, Shane decided to study the bible on his own.

As Shane made that life transforming decision to read the Bible, he came to a passage in Matthew 7:7-8 that says: *"Ask and it shall be given you; seek and you will find; knock and it will be opened to you. For everyone who asks receives, and he who seeks finds, and to him who knocks, it shall be opened."*

He took his questions to God, and boldly challenged God to reveal Himself the next day by 5 in the afternoon, otherwise he would choose to remain an atheist and never question atheism again.

To a lot of people, to challenge the Lord like this is like challenging the king to a duel. He gave God a deadline!

One might imagine God sitting on His throne with thousands upon thousands of angels straining themselves to send disaster upon this young, arrogant man. I recall the story in The Book of Job 38:2-3 when God answered Job from out of a whirlwind, which sends quivers down my spine each time I read this!

I can imagine God answering Shane with a thunder-like voice saying *"Who is this that darkens my counsel with words without knowledge? Brace yourself like a man. I will question you and you shall answer me!"*

Let us consider the greatness of God whenever we approach him. He is, after all, The Almighty God. Let's also consider the patience of God.

He saw that Shane was genuine in desiring to know the truth about God. God searches the heart and examines the mind. Sometimes, we fail to consider how deep His love and patience is. He desires that everyone come to repentance and know His Son Jesus Christ in whom we have salvation.

The following morning, forgetting the challenge he made with God, Shane went to work as usual, knowing nothing what God had in store for him.

During the course of the day, a radio broadcast talked about the prophecies of Nostradamus. I've got to hand it to his workmate who was sensitive to the nudge of the Holy Spirit and shifted the conversation to the gospel: *"Nostradamus isn't a 100 % right, but the Bible is,"* he remarked.

God used that simple statement to start the ball rolling. His workmate was a bit hesitant to open up because of that bold statement from Shane when he started. However, he sensed that Shane had a genuine interest to know.

He heeded the call of the Holy Spirit to share about the love of God, and the forgiveness of sins through the death of His Beloved Son Jesus Christ. It was the *first time* Shane heard the gospel message!

*"'Not by might, nor by power, but by My Spirit,' says The Lord Almighty"* (Zechariah 4:6). How big is The Almighty God? He

is El Elohim, the Creator of everything. He is the high and exalted One. He lives in a high and holy place (Isaiah 57:15). Consider His Glory, His eternality and transcendence. NOTHING is impossible with Him.

There was a disquieting moment, an epiphany that illuminated and filled Shane's thoughts. The conversation he had with his coworker lingered in his mind; however, his stubborn self-will *still* had to be shattered.

He attended a church service that Sunday night and the message at that time was on prophecies in Scripture. At the end of the service, the pastor asked if there was anyone in the congregation that wanted to surrender to Jesus Christ, and to raise their hand. Shane resisted telling himself that he wasn't going to do it, but he did! He raised his hand, not entirely by his own volition but by the power of the third person of the Godhead, the Holy Spirit!

The Holy Spirit moved Shane to bring into question his life, including the accidents. God had arranged circumstances for him to work among believers. He moved in the hearts of his fellow workers to share the gospel. God gave them wisdom on show to share around Shane. He emboldened his coworker to question Shane's belief, and another one to share the gospel clearly, which moved Shane's heart to heed the call, to raise his hand and go to the front and stand with all the others who had raised their hands.

His self-will was finally *shattered* and he came to the point of surrendering his life to Jesus Christ. Someone came to him and counseled him from the verse 1 John 1:9 *"If we confess our sins, He is faithful and just to forgive our sins and cleanse us from all unrighteousness."*

November 15 was Shane's day of surrender and he hasn't turned back ever since.

Life transformation is the fruit of a "crucified life".

Shane's a changed man, no longer angry at the world, so different from the man that used to drink and swear a lot. He found real peace and true conviction in God.

From atheism to faith in Jesus, what a giant leap for him! Yet because he found the truth, his purpose for living became clear. He decided to be a missionary in the Amazon tribal areas and was set on his goal of sharing the gospel to unreached tribes.

That sounded like martyrdom to me. To leave the paradise setting of the natural wonder that is New Zealand, and live amongst the tribal areas, where food and potable water are scarce, or face a hostile environment, is *unthinkable* for most.

But what we don't see is the heart of the Father. His desire *is* to see the gospel of Jesus reach even the remotest areas on earth. The mission to the Amazon tribe didn't push through and God's plan for Shane was made clear to him at a Christian camp in New Zealand.

There were two missionaries from the Philippines who spoke. The Philippines was unknown to him then, and didn't know any locals. He scuttled towards the wharf by himself and laid down to gaze at the stars. This was at a campsite in New Zealand.

I imagine the stars shined much brighter in that natural setting without the dazzling lights and the cacophony of sounds from the city. I imagine the night was tranquil and the dark velvet sky was a backdrop that showcased millions of sparkling stars.

This reminds me of the time in centuries past in the book of Genesis when God spoke to Abraham and put on display the magnificence of God's celestial objects. Shane must've felt the nearness of God during this time. He came before God in honesty and asked the Lord what He wanted for his life and to show him this weekend.

Over the weekend, God answered Shane by placing a burden on his heart for the Filipino people. He took this burden with him and brought it before the church eldership who responded favorably. "We were waiting for you to come to us about this!" they said.

Upon their recommendation, the plans of God for his life became clear. Before going to the Philippines to work as a missionary, his boss offered him a position that he had been eyeing before he came to know Jesus. I see Satan behind this, trying to stop him from obeying the call of God. Enticement is his game.

The lyrics of one of my favorite hymns just crossed mind: *"Turn your eyes upon Jesus. Look full in His wonderful face, and the things on earth will go strangely dim, in the light of His glory and grace"*.

Shane asked the Lord for confirmation regarding His plans for him. God spoke to him in Isaiah 43 and verse 4 came into focus: *"Since you are precious in My sight, Since you are honored and I love you, I will give other men in your place and other peoples in exchange for your life."* He got his confirmation from God. He packed up, left New Zealand and arrived in the Philippines on August 9, 1985.

Shane met his lovely wife Rene in the Philippines and they fell in love. This husband and wife team were part of the mission team when my husband and I first met them. We were searching for a home church and found a flyer that pointed to this small, nice setting.

During the time they were in Manila, Shane conducted bible studies almost every night and taught us the fundamentals of the Christian faith. We were so blessed to witness their diligence and vigor in proclaiming Christ.

Where did this passion come from? He recalled the time when he and his friend were going from house to house to distribute gospel tracts and were approached by a man with a knife. They were met with hostility and were asked to follow him to meet the Colonel. They had no inkling who this colonel was at the time, but they followed him anyway.

For whatever reason, the man became agitated and struck Shane's friend to the hilt of the knife without any provocation from them. I'm pretty sure that the gash was pretty deep, and he was most probably in agony and bleeding profusely.

Shane went to see the colonel with his friend holding his head, trying to keep calm. After they saw the Colonel, they were taken to the hospital afterwards. God is able to use unfortunate events such as this to accomplish His purpose.

The village officers became lenient to them and they were able to share the gospel to many homes. They were able to visit the man who struck his friend with the hilt of the knife and showed him forgiveness. He, together with his family, came to the saving grace of the Lord Jesus Christ!

As part of our training, Shane would bring us to a mall, each one with gospel tracts to distribute and talk to people about Jesus. We went from village to village distributing gospel tracts, meeting residents, and answering queries.

He set up bible studies even till late in the evening and we went to a public school to help lead bible studies with the teachers. This kind of training gave me greater passion in reaching out to people. It can be daunting at times especially when friends turn away because of one's faith, or humbling when one is faced with pruning or trials. Indeed, there is a cost to being a disciple of Jesus.

We press on, even in afflictions, rejections, and unfortunate events because God is with His servants. His purposes will prevail.

At times, His work will be accompanied with tangible miracles. There was an extraordinary occurrence that happened during an outreach program at the village's outdoor basketball court. It started to rain and after a few minutes, it poured. The amazing thing was, the basketball court remained dry, yet as soon as people stepped out of that dry patch, they would get soaked!

I can still picture this patch of land and remember that specific time when the Lord granted them to co-labor in His work to save people. That is an amazing picture of God's sovereignty and power.

There are several other miracles that follow His work, but the greatest miracle is seeing people come to the saving knowledge of the Lord Jesus Christ.

It is awe-inspiring to say the least to belong to the kingdom to God and witness the power of an awesome God. People focus on tangible occurrences, but the most important event is the life-altering faith that is only possible through the power of the Holy Spirit.

In hindsight, I can never forget the inspiration, the correction, gentle rebukes, training, the sound biblical teachings that were passed down to me, which I pass on to those that come after me in the faith.

Shane Wildermoth, once a scoffer of God and His people, is now a *relentless* worker for the Kingdom. His tireless efforts in proclaiming Christ caused us to pursue that path as well.

My husband and I regularly experience the joy of witnessing someone come to salvation in Jesus.

It is with great honor and pleasure that I have been tasked to write the story of workers in the faith. It is with humility and joy that I look forward to the day when I see the face of my Savior and Lord, Jesus Christ, as I bow before His throne amidst the heavenly beings that proclaim "Holy, Holy, Holy is the Lord God Almighty, the whole earth is full of His glory!"

*L→R: Their son Timothy, Leni, their daughter-in-law Nikki, their son Silas, Leni's husband Patrick*

# LENI HUFANA-DEL PRADO

Leni del Prado's passion lies in coaching, counselling and mentoring women and young people, so does her service to God and people from all walks of life.

Her wisdom and practical knowledge come from her introspective experience, exposure to different cultures, and interacting with people from all walks of life. She is a mentor to women, and though she wasn't trained in life coaching, some women gave her that title, as a personal life coach to them.

She and her Husband were restaurateurs at one point in their lives as they share the same love for culinary and travelling.

A graduate of The University of the Philippines, and a former title holder and first runner up of the Miss Philippines, she was ushered into a world of fashion modeling on the ramp and television commercials. She also acted and guested in television shows during her younger years.

She has been married for 31 years to Patrick F. del Prado. And she enjoys being a grandmother and is a proud mother of two grown men.

## CHAPTER 5

# The Journey Thus Far

By Ferdinand R. Gaite

Frankly, I never really imagined I would become a Congressman in the House of Representatives in the Philippines.

Not from a lack of ambition, but I just simply never thought I had the ability nor the wherewithal to occupy such a position.

I intentionally did not use "exalted" as an adjective to describe the word "position" for the perceived ill-repute attached to the "position" of Congressman.

Probably another subliminal reason why I never really aspired to be one.

I write because a group of my batchmates in high school wanted me to be part of this collaborative project, called RELENTLESS. Most of the Collaborative Authors of this book are graduates of the University of the Philippines Integrated School (UPIS) Class 1979.

And none of us would've been successful had we not been **relentless**.

From the roster of the Class of 1979 graduates, there are many illustrious members, to my mind, who could write much better lyrical prose and poetry, and have been given recognition for this in their respective fields and industries.

To name a few: Playwrite-philantrophist Jomar Fleras, Director-poet Floy Quintos, Editor-writer Carlo Tadiar, Theater artist-cyclist Jack Yabut, News reporter Ces Oreña-Drilon, and columnist JB Baylon.

But I had been asked by yet another distinguished alumnus of the Class of 1979 – Judge Amifaith Fider-Reyes, and I prelusively promised.

This is my story about being **relentless**.

It was in the second year of high school in 1975 when I met most of my batchmates at UPIS as a transferee from the International School. Mind you, being a transplant from a private school to a public school – was a *considerably* drastic change for me.

Allow me to recall what a big adjustment it had been for me.

Imagine the new environment that I faced. From the squeaky-clean, air-conditioned, well-furnished facilities and casual school clothes worn by the multinational population of the International School – I then shockingly encountered squeaking ceiling fans, pre-war wooden cabinets, graffiti-riddled wooden ancient armchairs, and white trubenized uniforms!

It was an eye opener – that the right to education was not exercised in the same terms.

And yet at the same time, it was at UPIS, where I met my memorable teachers and even more memorable friends. One of them even became my wife and the mother of my children, but that's another story.

Overall, I reminisce high school with fondness. The good, the bad and everything in between.

And as I look back, I wouldn't have traded places with anyone, for *anything*. I am proud to be a part of the UPIS Batch 79!

What brought me there, to a place some call *"the place of ill-repute"* – is the story that I wish to share.

This is a question that I have been asked several times, when interviewed by the media and even my high school classmates: How did I turn out to be a "rabble-rouser," a "political activist," a "unionist, a "leftist," an "anti-imperialist," and an "anti-whoever-is-in-power"?

Sometimes, I have also been called *worse* names.

Well, my parents and the years under the Marcos dictatorship definitely shaped my political awakening.

The transformation came at the young age of 10, while I was transfixed, watching live news being broadcast each evening, on our Zenith-brand, black-and-white TV, with my father, whom I fondly call Papa.

The day was August 21, 1971 – the horrific **Plaza Miranda bombing** occurred. A crowd of about 4,000 Filipinos were gathered to listen to speeches of the Liberal Party politicians who were on the stage. The Liberal Party had been the political opposition to the incumbent President in 1971, Ferdinand Marcos.

Two grenades were reportedly tossed onto the stage, and the entire lineup of candidates from the Liberal Party for the national elections suffered *unspeakable* injuries. The Plaza Miranda bombing caused nine (9) deaths and ninety-five (95) injuries.

Thankfully, the color-free broadcast had lessened what could have been the gore of it all.

I was deeply shocked at the carnage! It was so atrocious, I remember asking my father, in Pilipino, *"What is happening? Is that really the state of affairs in our country?"*

My dad was outraged!

He believed that Ferdinand Marcos was responsible for the violence. My Papa explained that Marcos knew that he would have *never* won the election, and wiping out his opposition was the *only* answer. Dumbfounded and angered, it was my first realization of the ugly face of our political arena.

From that defining moment onward, I remember that my hunger for political views became insatiable.

I remember competing with my dad to get first rights to the daily newspapers – **The Manila Times** and the **Free Press**, and not just for the comics section.

During meals, I remember asking him about a variety of things which I had read about, but, which I did not understand. My father explained them with the patience and trust that only a father could to a son.

Of course, I knew that he had named me after President Ferdinand Marcos, because when I was born, the latter had been a popular and charismatic leader at the time.

Later on, having taken to humor, I would joke that I had been named instead after Ferdinand Magellan, the Portuguese explorer who had allegedly discovered the Philippine islands in 1521. I refused to associate my being named "Ferdinand" with President Marcos.

My privileged bourgeoisie world in the cosmopolitan environment of the International School had likely dulled my political angst. Also, like most Filipinos who had grown up in a bilingual educational environment, my knowledge of the Filipino language suffered.

Truth be told, during my high school years at UPIS, Pilipino was one of my most dreaded subjects. And in many ways, not knowing the Philippines' national language – Pilipino –had deadened my sense of nationalism back then.

But attending UPIS for high school and then the University of the Philippines (U.P.) in college, left a significant influence on my life, and contributed in bringing back my political fervor. It had been a gradual awakening, though, as I did not initially see how taking my studies seriously would help me with the emerging political consciousness.

That was in 1979, as I entered college.

In their frustration with my performance in college, I remember my parents berating me, with, *"What will ever happen to the hope of the fatherland?"*, alluding to our national hero, Jose Rizal, who had referred to the youth as *"the hope of the fatherland."*

It was then that I was influenced and motivated to rethink about what I seriously wanted to do with my life. This significant time was in the year 1983.

That same fateful year, on August 12, 1983 – Benigno Aquino, Jr. also known as "Ninoy", a prominent oppositionist against President Marcos, was tragically assassinated.

It was exactly 12 years after the *frightful* scene at Plaza Miranda.

I realized that something had to be set right.

There was definitely something amiss. Marcos's cruel, heinous dictatorship, the brutal killings and Ninoy Aquino's assassination could never exist side-by-side with democracy and the sanctity of life.

The political atmosphere after Ninoy Aquino's assassination helped me to decide what I wanted out of life.

After transferring to another university – Lyceum of the Philippines – in 1983, I vowed to be **relentless** and more serious about my studies, while simultaneously becoming active in the student movement.

With this perseverance, the trust I gained from my fellow-students, and the consternation of the school administration, I was elected President of the Lyceum Central Student Council in 1984.

After that, I became heavily involved in other people's movements in the fight to oust the Marcos dictatorship under the newly-founded *Bagong Alyansang Makabayan* (literally "'New Patriotic Alliance'") in 1985.

Around this time, I married a batchmate from high school, Debbie Perez, in 1987. We have four great children: Karlo, Nina, Ado and Karina. And although it did not work out for us and have parted ways, we still remain friends.

After my college graduation, I decided to work at the Overseas Workers Welfare Administration (OWWA) in 1987, a government agency.

I literally rose from the ranks, starting first as a casual employee, and finally, as a Division Chief. I also became involved with public sector unionism serving as the president of the OWWA Union and as vice-president of the Department of Labor and Employment Employees Union.

For over two (2) decades, I served as the National President of the Confederation for Unity, Recognition and Advancement of Government Employees (or COURAGE). Its advocacy was for a decent living wage, humane conditions of work, security of tenure, as well as the people's political, economic and democratic rights.

In 2019, BAYAN MUNA (translation: the People First), a political party in the Philippine legislature, decided to have public sector workers represented in the House of Representatives. To my delight and rich satisfaction, they chose me as a nominee in the partylist elections.

BAYAN MUNA successfully obtained enough votes to place the maximum of three seats in the 18th Congress of the House of Representatives, together with human rights lawyer Atty. Carlos Zarate, and an indigenous people's leader Eufemia Cullamat.

This is how I became a Congressman in the House of Representatives in the Philippines.

This has been the journey thus far.

It still feels surreal. But, the task of pushing for the workers' and peoples' agenda is still down the road.

I cannot end this article without thanking my family, my friends in high school and college, my comrades in the people's movement, and all those who placed their trust and support to BAYAN MUNA and the principles we stand for.

And last, I have to give thanks to my father and my mother, for having instilled in me these values that formed who I am today.

As a point of clarification, I remain, *not* the "hope of the fatherland." Instead, **we** all are the hope of the fatherland.

*L →R Congressman Ferdie Gaite with fellow-Lyceum alumnus Joselito Alisuag*

# Ferdinand R. Gaite

Congressman Ferdinand Gaite is a member of the Philippine House of Representatives. He is currently one of the three representatives of the Bayan Muna Partylist in the elections of May 13, 2019 election.

He went to the University of the Philippines Integrated School, the University of the Philippines, and the Lyceum of the Philippines, for his formal education. But his education was completed in the streets, so to speak.

His advocacies include Workers' Rights especially migrants' welfare, and the protection of human rights under the current administration. He was married to Debbie Perez, the mother of his children, all of whom comprise his joy and treasure.

# CHAPTER 6

# The Sunflowers Grow Even After Summer

By Maria Josephine Trono-Lumawig

Each one of us has a unique place in life, different from others, destined by God, for His purpose, not for ours. Even as we push for what we want, **relentless** as we can be, life will always follow God's timing and direction.

We want life to be the way we plan it to be. We want celebrations to happen when we want them to happen. But God's *relentless* love for us, to give us true joy and peace in our unique place in life, will *allow* changes that we may *never* expect to happen.

The changes He allows in our lives will be relentless, just like His love for us. Indeed, so relentless that no one can ever stop these changes from happening.

No one can stop Him from loving us because He is God and He has a purpose for our lives. And because He is God, the *best celebrations* come from Him.

Romans 8:28 has been my life verse ever since I understood about God's unconditional love for man. *"And we know that all things work together for good to those who love God, to those who are the called according to His purpose."*

I held on to that verse as a young Christian because I wanted to remind myself of the assurance that whenever certain events happened in my life, it is God who allowed these to happen. And that He, being the best Artisan, is able to weave the tattered yarns together to complete a beautiful tapestry that will tell a beautiful story.

As I became older, sunrise after sunrise taught me that this tapestry was not about myself. That tapestry was about God relentlessly loving me, creatively and gently weaving it for His glory, for His purpose.

Changes in life pointed me back to that tapestry, woven through life's changes – phase after phase. Yarns, tattered as they seemed to be, can be woven intricately, producing interesting textures, in His perfect time, as long as the Perfect Artisan is the one on the loom. And because of this, life calls for my **relentless** trust and obedience to the Perfect Artisan, while He weaves my story.

I am presently a professor in a University. Becoming a teacher was *long* overdue. I had wanted to be one ever since I was in preschool. That was not a surprise since my Daddy and Mommy were both teachers. My Daddy taught college botany at the University where I teach now, while my Mommy taught high school biology at another university.

I grew up with teachers as parents. No wonder I had always wanted to be a teacher. But I never became one...*until* I was in my mid-forties! I tried my best not to be one. And yet God has good plans.

Last Night's Downpour

When I was six, I went to the same school where my Mommy taught.

I still remember the smell of the waxed paper that Mommy used to cover our notebooks, and the smell of the Pentel pen ink to label the notebooks with my name. The waxed paper cover had the same color as a brown paper bag, with one side waxed and shiny and the other side matte.

I remember one time when I watched Mommy prepare our notebooks a few weeks before the start of classes.

I stared at how she cut the waxed paper with a sharp pair of scissors and as the blades of the scissors pressed through the waxed paper, and that wonderful scent was released. It was the scent of the waxed paper, similar to the scent of burnt brown sugar, almost. After she cut the waxed paper, she would cover the notebooks and tape its edges with clear tape. Then I would excitedly wait for her to pull off the cap from the Pentel pen and as the tip of the pen touched the waxed paper, there was this heavenly scent that made me high.

One day, when she was supposed to write my name, I saw her write an 'L', then an 'E', and by the time she wrote a 'T', she suddenly stopped! We both realized that she was writing her name, **Letty**, on my notebook! But my clever Mommy continued and wrote **"Let It Be"**, the title of a popular Beatles song!

She wouldn't replace the waxed paper cover even if she had made a mistake…likely because it would've been such a waste. Or perhaps such a 'mistake' was for good. Besides, I really didn't mind. With my name below "Let It Be", I felt proud, like I was a Beatle!

Every school opening marked by the smell of the waxed paper and the pentel pen ink almost assured me a medal at the end of the school year. I was very proud to always be at the top of my class. I was never below the top three from kindergarten until first year high school.

I knew I studied well and was very good in school. The medals proved it.

I even repeatedly won in declamation and oratorical contests. I was proud to make my family proud. I was *good*, I whispered to myself. I didn't realize then I was merely going through the motions in desperation, hoping to always win and to always give my family reasons to be proud of me, fearing that one day I might fail them. It was a *tiring* routine, always working hard with the sole motivation of *pleasing people*.

While in Grade 6, I hoped to transfer to the University high school where my eldest brother, Edgar, graduated from – the same University where my Daddy was a professor.

I was in so much despair when my sister, Maret, and I *failed* the entrance exam. I thought I was intelligent enough to be able to pass, but unfortunately, I wasn't.

I remember crying hysterically, throwing my pillows around the bed when I learned I did not pass the exam. I heard my Mommy ask my Daddy if he could talk to someone from the University and somehow ask if something could be done so we could be admitted. My Daddy's answer was simple, *"I will not lift a finger. They did not pass, so they will not study there."*

I continued studying at my old school, and again finished first year high school *with honors!* Then I learned there were open slots for second year high school at the University High School, so my sister and I took the entrance exam for the second time and we both passed! So, I entered the University high school as a second-year student.

My first day in the new high school was *sorrowfully* memorable. My classmates were like gods and goddesses when they opened their mouths to introduce themselves. I was stunned how confidently they spoke English.

I heard one classmate say, "I was a five-oh-niner." I panicked picking the pieces of my brain from the floor trying to grasp what that word meant. I later realized 1-509 was a section in first year.

School life changed abruptly. I felt like a second-rate student.

I developed good friendships with a handful of personalities, though. We were *all* introverts – silent and shy – making silent, but fun memories together.

Whenever I try to recall memories from my second to fourth year high school, it almost seems like watching a silent movie. We were quiet, *even* in our laughter. But that was nice and sweet.

Slowly, I changed a bit from a shy high school girl to someone who loved to express herself. I capitalized on my long wavy hair, with boys calling me one of Charlie's Angels. It was the mid 1970's, and "Charlie's Angels" was in!

I knew those boys were merely teasing me rather than grooming me for stardom. But because rock stars back then had long wavy hair, I sort of had an identity. Now I had a reason to wear faded denim jeans with a patched seat and tattered bell- bottomed hems, paired with my white school uniform blouse. Yes, that was our uniform – a white blouse with big blue buttons at the center front and denim jeans. Sometimes, we would even wear wooden clogs! It was a far cry from my well ironed blouse, pleated skirt, necktie, black shoes and white socks from my elementary years.

As I progressed through my high school years, I learned to love rock and roll.

My older brother, Romy, had a rock band and I decided that rock music was good for me. The drums and the base guitar somehow gave me energy and excitement! Led Zeppelin was very popular that time. Their concert-movie "The Song

Remains the Same" opened in Manila and my classmate, Ven, and I went to see the movie.

And so, here's a confession – we cut classes *that* afternoon because of rock music.

When we entered the movie house, I felt intimidated because the crowd was quite rowdy. Ven and I were able to find seats somewhere in the middle of the orchestra section. As soon as we sat down, men from the balcony were throwing coins at us! A coin hit me on my head and another one on my knee. I froze and didn't know how to react. I was scared! I was not used to a rowdy crowd.

The crowd got noisier and I felt they were getting out of control. Ven and I decided to **bolt** out of the movie house! We were like laughing and almost crying at the same time. The worst part was once outside the building and under the sunlight, we realized we were wearing our uniforms, watching a rock concert, in broad daylight!

Somehow these changes – from an honor student to a second-rate student, from a clean-cut girl to feeling like a rock n roller – taught me that I can't always get what I want – such as medals and awards in school, which always made me proud of myself.

This new status at school made me focus more on friendships and on being humble. Yes, one thing that this change in status at school gave me was *appreciating* how others did far much better than me.

I later learned to be happy just being a 'good' average student with a few sweet, quiet friends alongside as I walked down the corridors. It was satisfying to be at peace, knowing I was different from them and that I didn't have to prove anything.

At high school graduation, many of my classmates went up the stage to get their medals for being honor students. I did not.

It was very different from my previous life back in my elementary years. I was a bit sad because I felt I did not make my family proud. But even then, I felt someone pat my back and I thought that it was fine. I gained a handful of loyal friends, the quiet kind, just like me, and somehow it released me from the desperate run to prove something.

While part of me was feeling a little envious, I felt the freedom of being a simple, quiet young lady who loved rock music. I spent most of my high school days embracing the realization of how much life *could* change.

I did not fully understand all these things because I had a limited perspective about life. While I knew there was a God, I didn't understand how things fit together. All I knew was there were changes in life and somehow, I had the ability to recognize these changes and just accept how these changes affected me. But I didn't have a deeper perspective why these changes happened. I didn't know God was continuously working out things, causing changes in my life, for me to learn to obey Him.

College was waiting for me and I wanted to be an architect. Oh wait, I thought I wanted to become a teacher, just like my Daddy and Mommy? Did that change?

I think I might have set that aside in my mind because I was told I couldn't earn a decent living as a teacher. I passed the University Entrance exams, enlisted in Bachelor of Science Architecture program and proudly met my classmates.

My beginnings in college were not very tough except for moments of insecurity when it was time to do our illustration activities in class. My classmates were *very* good at it. As for me, I could barely create shadows with my drafting pencil.

When our professor asked us to go around the campus and look for a building to sketch, I would go alone, and refused to show my work to anyone, except to my professor.

He questioned why ladies like me (there were only four girls in class) would want to be architects when architecture was for men. He even stressed that if we wanted to be successful, we had to come from a rich family.

That hit me bullseye! I was *not* from a rich family. I pretended not to hear what he said, but the thought banged inside my mind.

I withdrew from reality to sketch my feelings *in words*.

I was sad and felt alone because my female classmates were rich. I felt left out of the group, desperate, hoping for a way out. Had I chosen the wrong course?

Because of the loneliness, I wrote poems in the classroom while waiting for our professor to arrive. I'd separate myself from my classmates and write. From then on, I would write my diary in poetry, with only my small, pink diary notebook patiently listening to my stories.

Things became nastier in the Architecture program. That professor was pushing the ladies out of the program, so I started to look at the possibility of shifting to another course.

I heard about the B.S. Clothing Technology (BSCT) program at the College of Home Economics. I wasn't *that* interested in clothing, but I thought it was a good idea.

The garment industry back then was practically booming and I felt it was a good way to get a job right after graduation. I applied as a shiftee and was admitted.

This was where I finally felt at *home*. Perhaps because this **was** the College of *Home* Economics.

This was where I learned how to make my own clothes and weave my own fabric. This was where I gained good friends, many of whom are my closest friends to this day.

I vividly remember one night when we were finishing our weaving project at the basement of a bungalow, which was converted into a classroom, when suddenly the power went out.

It was pitch dark. We panicked and recklessly ran up the stairs, grappling with the steps, shrieking like little girls. There were ghost stories about this bungalow, and the situation was terrifying!

We suddenly remembered that one of our classmates was left inside the toilet. She was likely able to hurriedly pull up her underwear because to our surprise, she was suddenly running right behind us...probably still leaking.

I recognized then that college life could be fun *after all*, even if one didn't know how to sketch a building *or* wasn't rich. I really felt at home.

I cannot remember a sad day when I was in BSCT. Life was so light and jolly.

As I write, happy memories flood through my mind: my best friend and I singing *"Sa Kabukiran"* (In the Countryside) on the rooftop of the College of Business Administration, snacking with my pattern-making classmates on fried *"lumpiang togue"* (a type of egg roll) with matching chili vinegar along the corridor of the College of Home Economics, and giggling during our French laboratory class when one of our classmates called our true-blooded French instructor's name as Monsieur Cahoots instead of Monsieur Catuhe!

I had never laughed as frequently, prior to my BSCT days. You see, I grew up as a serious girl running for honors in grade school, and a quiet rocker in high school. I became a laughter-filled, carefree college girl.

I completed my college degree without delay even though I had shifted from B.S. Architecture to B.S. Clothing Technology.

I even received academic recognition, a small pin, for graduating with honors, which I never aimed for.

It had been seven long years since I'd received an academic award. What a pleasant surprise, like a gift for no occasion!

The bonus of graduating from the B.S. Clothing Technology program was that there were jobs waiting for us even when we *hadn't yet* graduated. BSCT graduates were in demand during the 1980s!

## Making Beautiful Things Possible

While I had fun in college, I'd always wondered why I never had any boyfriend. I knew I wasn't so pretty, but I saw girls who were just like me but had one boyfriend after another.

Ever since I was a young girl, I'd always wanted to have my own family. I pegged age 25 was the right time to get married, have kids, with a strict requirement for a three-year courtship. That meant by age 22, I had to have a serious boyfriend.

I was 20 when I graduated from college and no sign of a boyfriend.

That was the time when I planned to study in the United States. Forget about getting married at 25 years old! I could focus on further studies abroad.

I passed the necessary exams to land a scholarship at a few universities in U.S.

There was also this *one* exam that friends told me was quite difficult and I had to review for.

On June 3, 1988, I took a leave from my work. It was 7:00 a.m. on a drizzly Friday morning. I waited for my turn to ride the Makati-bound **Love Bus** – a popular airconditioned bus painted with large pink and red hearts.

There was a queue of passengers waiting for the next empty Love Bus to arrive. I saw this stocky man in a black leather jacket, about five to seven passengers behind me in the line. When the bus arrived, I hopped in and took a comfortable seat by the window.

A few minutes after settling on my seat, this stocky guy in the black leather jacket, climbed into the bus, sat two seats behind me, then *suddenly* transferred about four seats in front of me. I rolled my eyes and murmured in alto voice, *'He does not know which seat to take.'*

Suddenly, by some kind of a force, he stood up again and decided to sit right beside me! As he did, his black leather jacket brushed my grey cotton fleece sweatshirt, giving me goosebumps behind my neck. It was cold because of the rainy weather…that was it, I thought.

I closed my eyes, thinking I would sleep the entire trip to Makati, about an hour's ride. Yet I sensed this guy kept looking down at me while I was sleeping and that made me self-conscious.

Without warning, my stomach started rumbling – I had to

eat something. I reached into my bag and took out a bar of Nestlé Crunch.

As I was about to remove the wrapper, this guy looked down at my chocolate and I got slightly pissed off and with much courage I sarcastically asked him, "Would you like some?" Well, he said, "No," but he started a conversation and it felt good.

He talked about how he watched the breakwater by the Manila Bay the day before while it was raining. I did not give him much information about myself except for my nickname and last name and that I worked at Shoemart (one of the largest department stores).

The ride went by quickly. I got off the bus in front of the Thomas Jefferson Library to review for my exam.

Well, from that day, my plans to study in the U.S. were permanently aborted because three years after that Makati-bound Love Bus ride, and after *three years of courtship*, I married Francis, the stocky guy in the black leather jacket who sat beside me one drizzly Friday morning.

That sudden change of plans – from plans to study abroad to getting married, came effortlessly. I fell in love and was finally going to live my dream of having my own family!

He was 29 and I was 28 when we got married. Having our own children was a fulfillment of *our* dreams. We had Francis Joshua, in 1992, Francesca Joanna in 1997, and two more surprises, in 2006 and 2008. We had a simple life moving from one house to another, including a small house we bought. Alongside a growing family, I had a swinging career.

My first job was in 1983, only a few months after graduation, before I met Francis. I was a production assistant in a garment manufacturing company which served a high-end ladies sleepwear label in New York. I lasted 15 months in that company. Being a fresh graduate, I found the work *highly* stressful due to the fast-paced production timeline that we had to keep.

In the last quarter of 1984, I left that company and started working at Shoemart as a Merchandise Researcher. This was such a happy job for me. My boss, Patty, was my former professor and I loved her like an older sister.

I enjoyed doing research on, and teaching salesclerks the different selling points of *new products*. I felt joy in teaching the salesclerks. I thought I might have loved being a teacher but then I needed to earn enough for a living. My five years at Shoemart were very happy. I met Francis while I was working there. I worked there for five years until I had a higher paying job in 1989.

The next 15 years saw me working at two companies, as a garment export merchandiser for a UK-affiliated multinational company headquartered in Hongkong for five years, and as one of the garment export merchandiser pioneers for a Chinese-owned multinational company, believed to be the biggest trading company in the world at that time – where I grew my career for 10 years.

Finally, in 2004, I was offered a job by a former workmate who started her own garment trading business. Even though I was getting tired of the stress in the garment industry, I accepted the attractive salary offer.

I felt I was in a secure place, at the peak of my career, believing that I was getting a slightly bigger salary than the average BSCT graduate of my age. I was Senior Export Garment Merchandiser for a New York girl's dress label. It was a taxing job with New York buyers calling the office late at night with demands left and right, and with quality control inspectors coordinating with me before midnight to report problems that needed fixed before shipment cut off came in a few hours.

On top of that, a boss who was most of the time yelling at everyone, made the job more challenging. It *wasn't* a happy job. I wanted to quit but couldn't because I felt there was nowhere to go. It was a torturous situation for me, having to deal with a difficult person at work.

Well, I brought home that torture and was messing up my family life. My marriage experienced a temporary twist and Francis and I had to deal with very challenging issues.

But God was gracious, *truly* gracious to us. I was *43 years old* when I got pregnant with our third baby, Francine Joy Grace. Then like a wonderful "joke", after a year, I got pregnant *again* and had Frances Jordine when I was *45!*

Stress from my boss affected me more. I remember being left alone in our office at the 21st floor at past 10:00 in the evening, with my pre-labor cramps, with an order to wait for the call from New York.

Providentially, I felt God rescue me from the work stress when He allowed a potential miscarriage at about four weeks into my pregnancy. My doctor suggested that I resign from the job to keep the baby. I did, *immediately*.

Reflecting now on those days confirms that the Lord caused many of these things to happen to rescue me out of my work in the garment industry. It was only the *"threatened abortion"* that caused me to let go of something that I thought made me secure.

Being a more mature Christian, I was *certain* it was Him. Soon after I resigned, after a few weeks of rest, Jody was well, strong, and growing inside me.

But for the very first time, I was *jobless*. I was praying for a job, something new and fresh. Then God called.

In April of 2008, the month I was going to give birth to Jody, my former professor in College and former boss at Shoemart in the mid 1980s, Patty, called me out of the blue and offered me a teaching job in the BS Clothing Technology program! I had *no* doubt that this was a Divine call. The application process was smooth, with an interview at home, because I was having early labor contractions. The Lord allowed me to get accepted for the job even *without* a teaching demo, which was quite *unusual*.

A few weeks after delivering Jody, I reported for work as a

full-time faculty member, with my former professor and boss, Patty, as my colleague.

However, our working together was short-lived because Patty passed on, due to an illness about two years after I started in the academe. I was considerably sad when she died. I felt like a little child left alone in a noisy theme park.

The Lord had other plans. This was the point in my life when I clearly saw that God uses circumstances and people to lead me to the path, He truly planned for me to take. Even with my self-controlled compass, finding my own way through my career, He and His *relentless* way of directing me to His path was very evident at this time.

It was time to trust and obey.

## Even After Summer

I was already 45 when I started teaching. That was late, compared to the other co-faculty in my Department. I felt somewhat awkward. All of the other teachers started in the academe very early, some right after or only a few years after graduation. I felt like a cosmos flower among sunflowers, a beginner among seasoned professors.

As of this writing, I've been teaching for 12 years now. Looking back, my years in the academe rocked-and-rolled pleasantly. I felt I belonged here, career-wise at least.

Even when financially short at many times, I easily settled down and felt I had a very warm connection with students.

While my plans years ago to take graduate studies abroad was aborted due to that Love Bus ride with the stocky guy in the black leather jacket, God gave me the opportunity to take my Masters in Education *this* time.

I succeeded with my studies, graduated with an 'Academic Excellence Award' for which I received a medal…something I'd "habitually" received during my grade school years. The award came as a surprise.

*This* time, I didn't sense that it was about making my family proud. *This* time, I felt it was **God's** pat on my back, assuring me that I was on the path He'd prepared for me. It signified a reward for my obedience to His relentless love and patience in showing me His directions.

## The Sun Brings New Beginnings

Earlier in my years of teaching, the annual graduation ceremonies took place in April, the peak of summertime in Manila. Graduates, wearing their ceremonial Filipiniana dress and "Sablay" (graduation sash), together with their families, would pose for pictures amidst the field of blooming sunflowers along the main road by the entrance of the University.

Every year during the graduation season, professors, students, and visitors would take their pictures surrounded by cheerful sunflowers. It was an iconic scene in pictures flooding my Facebook feed *every* graduation season.

The University Community Maintenance team would plant the sunflowers in the campus, along the main road by the university entrance, and around the Amphitheater where the commencement ceremonies were held. They would begin planting the sunflowers during the start of summer so that they'd be in full bloom during Graduation day. Residing inside the campus gave me the chance to witness every inch of progress in the growth of the sunflowers on a yearly basis.

All this changed in 2014. The University shifted its academic calendar. From the usual start of classes in June, the first semester now ran from August until December, and the second semester from January until May.

This shift moved the graduation day from April to June. It meant losing the traditional summer break *matching* the summer days; instead, the annual school year break would start during the rainy season! And oh yes, it also meant delaying the planting of the sunflowers by *two* months! Oh no, that sounded more like planting **rainflowers** instead of **sunflowers**!

These days the sunflowers start to sprout and bloom when the rainy season begins. Whenever heavy rains pound the grounds overnight, I get anxious and wonder if the sunflowers would survive.

In fairness, the first June graduation season went well. Imagine, the ceremonies were spared from the rains. And the sunflowers still bloomed…what a lovely change!

For years now in the University, the sunflower has been a symbol of graduation, of celebration, of happy endings and of new beginnings, a color of success and of future challenges. It has remained as that until now, but probably with a slightly different meaning.

## When the Rains Come

It was the midterm of the second semester of 2020 when the quarantine started due to the COVID 19 pandemic. Being quarantined in our house, inside the school campus since March, I seldom went out, except maybe for a few times when I had to buy what they call "the essentials."

As I write this book chapter, I realized that it has been over six months today since the quarantine began. To say that there has been a lot of changes recently is an *understatement*. Things have changed, *greatly* changed.

This year, 2020, was very different.

The pandemic has affected lives all over the world, including our little graduation tradition. The pandemic changed how things have been. There was no usual Commencement exercises in the Amphitheater, the way it has been since I started teaching 12 years ago.

I find myself crying many times, feeling sad about how the pandemic has spoiled a lot of things in University life.

I *do* miss my students a lot, their noise and laughter, our lively and many times, funny discussions in class. I miss presenting the course lessons in class and the moments of reflecting on life lessons with them.

I'm not sure though if my students realize that I learn a lot of worthy lessons from my interactions with them, too. This pandemic brought a lot of changes, a lot of moments of thinking about how life has been and how life will be.

One thing though that the pandemic did not stop was the campus maintenance team. Though about a month late, they still did plant the sunflowers along the main road by the entrance of the University, perhaps to signal the end of the academic year, and to continue the *sunflower tradition*.

Even without the Commencement Exercises in the Amphitheater, we were still able to send off our graduates virtually and cheer them with "Padayon!", a Visayan word which means "Go forward!"

## Finally, This We Need to Know

There are and will always be changes in life.

These changes will weave into life, making life not always how we have planned it to be. The celebrations we want to happen may not happen at the time when we want them to happen.

My past always reminds me that these changes happen because of God's *relentless love*. Some changes are drastic and immense, others are slow and hardly noticed.

Sometimes, because of shortsightedness, some changes are viewed as unfortunate. There are also changes that just do not seem to make sense like when our youngest sibling, Aloha, passed on in 2015 due to a massive brain aneurysm and her husband followed six months after, leaving behind their three daughters.

Nevertheless, I know that one day, when God's work in me is complete, I will fully understand why such events happen in life.

But all in all, my life has been a proof that changes through God's hands, without doubt, work together for good for those who love Him and are called for His purpose. And this, I hope to remind those whom I love – that changes, whether brought about by the sun or the rain, as long as we *relentlessly* stand, with obedience and trust, along the path prepared for us by the Almighty, will weave for Him a most beautiful tapestry.

*Finally, this we need to know –*
*the sunflowers grow even after summer.*
*As I listened to last night's downpour, I thought of the sunflowers.*
*I wonder if they will survive. I actually hope they will.*
*But then I thought, sunflowers are supposed to grow during summer.*
*They love the sun, almost intensely desiring it.*
*How can we ask them to bloom in June, when the rains come?*
*But God does have His ways of making beautiful things*

*possible, even at a seemingly wrong time, like making
sunflowers bloom even after summer.
After the rains, the sunflower turns its
face towards the sun, staring at it,
the source of its life.
It bends down when the darkness of night covers life.
But then again, it proudly raises up its
gaze as the sun rises in the morning,
knowing that the sun brings new beginnings.
Because change is relentless, we expect the darkness of nights
but we should be excited with the brightness of new mornings.
We should be like the sunflower, turning our gaze
to the source of life,
because every morning brings fresh beginnings.
Wherever life places us, whenever things
happen at a seemingly wrong time,
we remember that even sunflowers grow after summer.
There will never be a wrong time for us to do our best, to use
our talents, to serve others, and to make life beautiful.
Remember, because God's love is relentless, the
sunflowers grow even after summer.*

*Left to Right: Francis, Francine, Josephine, Frances, Francesca, Francis Joshua*

# Maria Josephine Trono-Lumawig

Maria Josephine Trono-Lumawig also known as "Jo" to her friends, was born in 1963 to two teachers, Jun and Letty Trono. She is the fourth of five children.

She went to the Manila Central University for her elementary years through first year high school and then to the University of the Philippines High School in Diliman, Quezon City for her second to fourth year high school.

She graduated in 1983 with a B.S. degree in Clothing Technology from the University of the Philippines (U.P.) in Diliman. She finished her M.A. in Education (Curriculum and Instruction) from U.P. Diliman in 2014.

She has been happily married to Francis for 29 years, and they have four children, Francis Joshua, Francesca Joy, Francine Joy, and Frances Jordine. She had a 26-year career in the garment industry until she went into academe, teaching in the B.S. Clothing Technology program for over 12 years now.

She believes in the God of the Bible, and her life verse is Romans 8:28.

## CHAPTER 7

# Relentless in Faith, Relentless in Hope, Relentless in Love

By Jackie Lansangan-Morey

"Three things will last forever—faith, hope, and love—and the greatest of these is love." 1 Corinthians 13:13 NLT

## Relentless in Faith

Has your faith ever been tested?

Can you recall a time in your life when you were unexpectedly plunged into the a dire situation, and you had no idea how you were going to come out on the other side…except through your faith in the LORD?

### The $35 test of faith

In April 1984, a few short weeks after we had both taken the *last* of **all** our college final exams, my sister Jen and I immigrated from the Philippines to the U.S.

The day before we flew out, our Dad generously handed me USD$1500 to help get us on our feet.

He told me, "I'm entrusting this to you – for you and your sister. After it runs out, I can't give you any more."

I acknowledged, "Ok, yes, Dad. Thank you very much!!"

The next day, we flew from the Philippines to Houston, Texas where our Aunt Grace and Uncle Vic graciously hosted us for about eight months in their home, and unsparingly lent us one of their cars so that Jen and I could begin looking for jobs.

Not only this, but Uncle Vic and Tita Grace only charged us for food, lodging and car insurance.

The rest of our money was spent on getting my driver's license, paying for gasoline, snacks or meals when we were out and about job hunting, stationery for our resumes, resumé printing, envelopes, stamps, long-distance calls, and other necessities.

Jen and I had opened a savings account shortly after we had arrived, so that we could access the $1500 Dad had given us, via ATM cards.

Well, about *five months* later, I went to the bank to withdraw more money to pay our gracious aunt and uncle.

After I had cash in hand, I checked our balance on the ATM transaction receipt and discovered that our $1500 had *dwindled down* to a mere $35.00!!

Here we were – in a new country, with our parents over eight thousand miles away, unable to help, and only a small amount of money left.

And though Jen and I had gone on several interviews, we were both *still* jobless.

At that moment, still standing close to the ATM machine, I decided *not* to tell Jen that we only had $35 to our name – because I didn't want her to worry.

Also, after I made that decision, I prayed a quick prayer to the Lord, "Father God, You see that we only have $35 left, You know that Jen and I still don't have jobs, You know that Dad won't give us any more money, You know where we are, You know where we live, and I know that You care for us. I trust you, Lord. Please help us to find jobs very soon."

Shortly thereafter, I told Jen that we needed temporary jobs just to tide us over until we found more permanent jobs.

I also remembered what my Dad had said before we left the Philippines, "Don't hesitate to take any job at first. As long as you're not stealing from anyone, or doing something illegal, don't despise even menial jobs."

So, even without my telling Jen about our meager $35 balance, we both applied for jobs at nearby Dairy Queen (DQ) locations.

DQ is a multinational fast-food company that serves ice creams, sodas, burgers and fries.

A few days later, we *both* got jobs at different DQ locations!!

No matter how menial our jobs were, we served our customers to the best of our abilities.

And even though we were college graduates, we *didn't* despise our work there. Instead, we were grateful for GOD's provision in the interim.

Incredibly, *less than a month* after we first started working at DQ, Jen and I both found permanent jobs…praise GOD!!

Here's the bottom line…

From the moment I learned about our $35 balance on the transaction receipt, to the time Jen and I found temporary jobs at DQ, up to the week we both got our first permanent jobs, my faith *not only* remained steady, but it marvelously grew by leaps and bounds!

Since that time in 1984, because of this $35 test of faith, I can attest that I got to *know* GOD as my sole Provider, my only true Source of provision.

I got to know HIM as Jehovah-Jireh – my generous, faithful and trustworthy Father GOD Who provides for all of my needs according to His riches in Christ Jesus!!

And ever since that short season some decades ago, I have **not** worried regarding money issues because I've *known* GOD as my Jehovah-Jireh.

I *know* that HE will always provide for all of my needs, and I *know* that HE will never fail me.

Ever.

## The $6,000 Shock

One afternoon in 2010, my Husband Jim and I were happily talking as I was going through our stack of mail, while he prepared something in the kitchen.

There was a large white envelope in the stack.

When I finally opened it and looked at its contents, my jaw dropped!!

It was an *unexpected* invoice from a lawyer, to the tune of $6,000!!

You see, we had hired an attorney to take care of some very important documents and arrangements for us.

We were very grateful for all that this lawyer had done.

We knew we would owe him *a few more* thousand dollars because after all, we had *already* paid him – in fact, over $4,000 previously.

So we knew we might owe him a little bit more.

We certainly *didn't* expect this large invoice coming.

At all.

Indeed, it *completely* took us by surprise!

As soon as I saw the bill, I fell silent because I knew we *didn't* have $6,000 in our account at that time.

I promptly showed my Husband the bill and at that moment, I had the choice to get very emotional, become upset and get tempted to take this out on my Husband.

But thankfully, I chose wisely…whew!

I calmly said to Jim, "Well, I'm not going to get upset. Instead, because you are the head of this household, I'm going to leave you for a few minutes so that you can figure out how we're going to pay this bill. I know that the Lord will provide."

It was *yet* another test of my faith, **and** Jim's faith.

I quickly recalled the $35 test of faith from 1984. So I knew beyond a shadow of a doubt that Father GOD would provide for us…somehow!

With this, I briskly walked upstairs to cool down and to give my Husband the time and the space to think, and to brainstorm about possible solutions.

While upstairs, I promptly exercised my faith as I prayed to the Lord, asking HIM to give Jim ideas on how we could pay the attorney.

Well, it didn't take long at all for GOD to answer.

To my delight and surprise, Jim ran up the stairs only *a few minutes later* and conveyed that the LORD had given him a solution – our tax returns!

What?!

I asked him to explain.

He said that the Lord given him the idea to look again at our last two years of tax returns and to re-file these, because he would soon discover that we had more money coming to us!!

Wow…really?!

Yes!

Indeed, there were items that we could look for, review, re-file and claim more money back.

This is exactly what Jim did for the next 48 hours.

Lo and behold, by the time he was done, Jim discovered <u>over $6,000</u> worth of items that we *hadn't* included in our last two years of filing our returns, that the IRS could refund to us…amazing!!

So we re-filed our taxes for the previous two years, and within a few weeks, received a refund check for *over* $6000, and promptly paid our attorney!!

Jim and I give *all* the glory to our faithful and trustworthy Father God for this $6,000 miracle.

Over the years that followed this test of faith in 2010, Jim and I have had *many other* tests of our faith.

Would our faith falter? Would our faith waiver? Would we trust in GOD?

Candidly, I can say that whenever our faith has been tested and dross that remained has risen to the surface, through HIM we have ultimately ended up increasing in our faith and trusting in the Lord even *more* than ever before.

You see, *HE* is the One Who has allowed us to go through *many* other different faith-tests over the years.

Why?

We believe that GOD's purpose and desire is that whatever tests come our way, and whatever tests come *your* way, by His Spirit – we can be RELENTLESS in *faith*.

## Relentless in Hope

### Ground Zero

The month was December 2014.

The church community that my family had attended for *years*, experienced a *bombshell* !

The Senior Pastor and his wife were asked to resign because what was brought to the light is that they had done abusive things and spoken terribly hurtful words over the course of *over* 15 years toward members of our community, *and* their children!

Sadly, their actions and words had *deeply* hurt scores of families – whose children had been attending the K-12 school that the church community had established.

Many of these children had grown up in this close-knit community since birth, and now, some were in their teens, others in their 20s.

My husband and I had *no* idea about any of these hurtful incidents and were spared from *much* of the devastation that others had painfully experienced, because both our children were too young to be part of the K-12 academy.

Unfortunately, the Senior Pastor and his wife had created a culture of religious legalism, without the "amazing grace" that they often preached.

After the Senior Pastor turned in his written resignation, families left the church community *in droves!*

Hundreds felt deeply wounded, emotionally abused, often manipulated, and now they refused to have anything more to do with "church".

My Husband and I were profoundly shocked, and couldn't believe how quickly the entire thing unraveled right before our eyes.

The remaining pastors and elders did their best to stop the hemorrhaging, but it was too late because the damage was deep and wide.

My Husband and I continued attending Sunday services. We waited with expectation and *hope* for several more months to see if our community would grow.

But week after week, the atmosphere in the community didn't change much. It certainly wasn't the same as it had been before December 2014.

In fact, it was *never* the same again.

Then in early December 2015, another "bombshell" occurred when our Pastoral leadership announced that on December 24, 2015, the Christmas Eve service would be the *final* service of our church community – numbering in the sparse hundred or so who remained.

They also conveyed that on December 31, 2015, the church entity would *cease to exist!*

*That* was the final blow.

Our small community was devastated.

We had held on to **hope** for *over a year*.

**Hope** that our community would recover.

**Hope** that the families who had been hurt would somehow return, now that the former Senior Pastor and his wife who had hurt them were no longer a part of the community.

Well, our *hopes* were dashed.

Why didn't those who were hurt, ever return?

After all, the Senior Pastor and his wife who had dreadfully wounded them were *gone!*

Perhaps because the foundation of the community was faulty.

Maybe the foundation had been *irreparably* damaged, and the Lord wanted it "razed to the ground"…this way, we could all start fresh – *elsewhere.*

Whatever the reason, our *hopes* were crushed.

## The Fallout

In the months that followed, Jim and I learned some jaw-dropping, shocking and heart-wrenching stories about some of the things that the Senior Pastor *and* his wife, did and said to members of our community.

Most of it was emotionally abusive, manipulative, and mentally abusive. We could only imagine how soul-crushing, demoralizing, and quite disturbing this had been for those directly impacted by them.

It was so abominable, loathsome and detestable that it caused many, many family rifts.

For example, young adult children who had graduated from the K-12 Academy *refused* to have anything to do with GOD, shunned being involved with *any* church community, and kept their distance from *any* other church community their parents chose to belong to, after our church community blew out.

Others young adults completely turned their back on all the solid biblical truths they had learned since they were young children.

Many Husband-Wife relationships became incredibly strained resulting in marital problems.

Others ended up in divorce.

Why?

Perhaps because of *all* the undealt-with, unaddressed, deep emotional wounds that had been inflicted on *them* directly and personally by the Senior Pastor and his wife.

Or maybe it was because watching their children completely turn away from the Lord added insult to injury, which caused more disillusionment and emotional devastation.

I don't know for sure. I can only surmise.

Now let me be clear. Our church community was made up of the most caring, hospitable, committed and Christ-centered people we had ever met. Our friendships were strong, deep and healthy, and had lasted for many years.

And yet *we* had all – yes, we and *all* our friends in the community – had *all* drunk the Kool-Aid. We rarely questioned the Senior Pastor or his wife because then they would label us "rebellious."

See how that worked?

So as a community, we *failed* to stop and discern. We *failed* to see clearly. We *failed* to listen to those outside our community. We *failed* each other. We *failed* our families. We *failed* our children. We *failed* our friends.

## Picking Up The Pieces

When the official church community entity ceased to exist effective December 31, 2015, my Husband and I were *crushed* and devastated.

It felt like our hearts were *shattered* into a thousand pieces.

Waves of grief and loss crashed over our souls, day in and day out. I personally entered into the new year 2016 – going through the ups and downs of the grieving process.

*How* in the world did we get here?

Was this going to be *our* story that marked the rest of our lives?

What good could *ever* come out of this terrible mess?

Candidly, there were certain weeks when I personally didn't attend any church services even when with my Husband and children went.

I simply didn't want to be around Christians because this would only remind me of the massive blowup back in December 2014, and the fresh, raw reality that our church community had *ceased to be*.

I felt emotionally worn out, devastated, and depressed…the grief and pain were wearing me out physically, such that I didn't want to do much of anything.

Was there any *hope* that I could get out of this pit of emotional devastation and grief?

Was there any *hope* that my Husband and I could belong to another strong, caring, loving community of believers again?

## Rise from the Ashes

After months of this, I shared with my Husband Jim that I needed outside intervention.

He admitted to me that he, too, needed healing from this *distressing* and excruciating experience.

Thankfully, we *both* agreed that we didn't want to stay in this place of grief and pain, we refused to stay stuck, and we both wanted to make forward progress.

So we decided that our inner healing process was to purposefully find a *Sozo* facilitator in our area.

*Sozo* is the Greek word which means "salvation."

The rich meaning of this word *sozo* doesn't only include the salvation of one's spirit; it also includes the *healing* and *salvation* of one's soul – one's mind, one's will, and one's emotions from excruciating emotional wounds.

In other words, Sozo means *"to be made whole."*

"To be made whole" especially after a person experiences deep pain, huge loss, emotional trauma, physical trauma, and even mental trauma.

And Sozo is a ministry that originated from Bethel Church in Redding, California.

[Note: Bethel Church has trained and mentored Sozo Teams from all over the world.]

After we found a Sozo Team – who happened to be at a church community over 3 hours away, my Husband and I made the trek to Port Angeles, Washington for our individual sessions.

We had no idea what would happen, since it was our very first Sozo session.

My Husband Jim had his session with two Sozo team members in one room, and I had my own Sozo session with two other team members in another room.

Oh my goodness!! What we each experienced during our individual two-hour Sozo sessions was extraordinary, glorious and astonishing!

The session absolutely also included actively and out-loud forgiving the Senior Pastor and his wife. It involved hearing what God was saying to us, and it also involved being immersed in GOD's presence the *entire* time!

Amazingly, I felt the weight of the grief and the low-grade pain of all the losses – all lift off from me. There's no question in my mind, that this was a supernatural experience, and I was free!

My Husband and I were both *healed in our souls*, and **free** – free from grief, free from the pain of deep, excruciating loss, and free to face the future with a renewed sense of *hope* and freedom.

Oh, Freedom.

And oh, to *hope* again…it was wonderful!!

What a remarkable, supernatural gift from the Lord!!

My *hope* that we could once again belong to a committed church community was not only restored, but in the years that followed, my hopes were fully realized.

The community that Jim and I are now a part of is beyond my expectations!

## Final Thoughts

From the depths of grief, pain and loss, from the gripping pain of failure, from questioning whether I could hope again – through the Lord, I have risen from the ashes – healed, set free and healthy once again.

Dear one – you can move the needle forward **from** failure, sorrow, and loss…**to** healing, deliverance, and freedom.

Whatever life throws your way, you can decide and commit to move from fear to freedom, from loss to supernatural gain, and from hope crushed to hope realized.

Yes, you can hope again.

And indeed, you, too – can become RELENTLESS in *hope*.

## Relentless in Love

"Love never gives up, never loses faith, is always hopeful, and endures through every circumstance." 1 Corinthians 13:7 NLT

### Love never gives up

Have you ever heard of marriages that lasted only 4 months and then ended up in divorce?

It always pains my heart whenever I hear of another divorce – whether the marriage lasted a mere four months or twenty four years. Divorce grieves me.

In this day and age when divorce remains an option and the choice for many couples, the marriage covenant and the vows they'd made are as *flimsy* as old, brittle paper or a very thin piece of cloth that easily tears!

> [**Note:** Now I'm *not* talking about a marriage wherein one spouse is physically abusive, or violent, or emotionally toxic, or has committed adultery – and is *unrepentant*. In

such cases, the Bible is clear that the victimized spouse may leave and divorce the abusive &/or adulterous spouse.]

Now that we're clear on our presuppositions, let's focus on the first part of 1 Corinthians 13:7 which says: "Love **never** gives up…" (emphasis mine)

Can you believe it? Love *never* gives up!!

In other words…

**Love is relentless!!**

Love doesn't give up when the going gets rough.

Love is *relentless* when tragedy hits or sickness occurs or trial after trial ensues.

One of the best examples that demonstrates that love is relentless – is a marriage that has *successfully* gone through *many* years of both wedded bliss – as well as trials, tests and tribulations, *and* the relationship between the husband and wife is stronger and deeper than ever before.

I've been privileged to have many examples of godly marriages that have lasted and gotten stronger over time, through all kinds of trials, sickness, and tribulations.

Some of these married couples have mentored my husband Jim and me when we were courting, when we got engaged, when we got married, and through the years that followed.

Now let me to tell you *two* short stories…one about my parents, and another one about a woman named Monica who lived a long time ago.

## Separated for Seven Years and 8,500 miles of Distance

In 1984, shortly after my sister Jen and I graduated from the University of the Philippines, Diliman, Quezon City – with our Bachelor of Science degrees, we made final preparations to move to Houston, Texas, over 8,500 miles away.

I can't even imagine the gamut of emotions my parents felt when they dealt with the reality that they would "lose" not just one, but *two* of their children to another country in one fell swoop!

On April 21, 1984, my sister Jen and I boarded a plane with our Grandma, for the first leg of our trip from Manila to Texas.

Because I was born in San Diego, California, I had a U.S. Passport. At that time, Jen did not. She had a tourist visa, and later, enrolled in classes and was on a student visa for many years.

We needed one of our parents to petition for Jen to become an immigrant here in the U.S. because it was a lot shorter than if I were to petition for my sister.

I want to acknowledge my Mom and Dad, because a year later, my parents agreed that my Mom would become an immigrant to the United States. Dad would remain in the Philippines to care for my 3 youngest siblings who were still in school.

My loving parents both decided that when I petitioned for Mom's resident status in 1985, Mom would live with me and my sister in Texas, until Mom could successfully petition my four other siblings, including Jen to become permanent residents in the U.S. – and until all these petitions were approved.

So, Mom lived with Jen and me for **seven long years**…apart from her husband for all those many, many months!!

*Indeed, parenting is not for the faint of heart.*

This was an incredibly considerable and lengthy time for my Mom and Dad to be apart!!

And yet, they both willingly chose this, and sacrificed being together for several years during this precious time in their lives – for the benefit of their children.

As you can see, *love is relentless!!*

After seven years, thankfully my sister fell in love, and ended up marrying her high school classmate who was already a U.S. resident.

And in that time frame, our 3 other Manila-based siblings decided that they *didn't* want to move to the U.S. after all!

So, Mom moved back to the Philippines shortly after Jen and Tong got married.

Oh how wonderful!! My parents were finally reunited proving that their marriage had **withstood** the *test of time* and the *trial of separation* – for the sake of their children.

Their love for each other was indeed *relentless*.

As I look back, I fully believe the Lord rewarded Mom and Dad for their astounding *sacrificial love,* by blessing them with *many* years of traveling together, enjoying the fruits of their labor, finally relishing and soaking up the many places and cultures all over the world – that they had both longed to visit together.

I thank the LORD that they were RELENTLESS in *love!*

## The Relentless Love of a Wife and Mother named Monica

Once upon a time, there was a woman named Monica who was from a moderately wealthy family. An old maidservant who had raised Monica's father, brought up Monica in the Christian faith.

Monica grew into a godly Christian who was later given in marriage to an unbeliever named Patricius.

For many years she tried to influence her husband to become a Christian, but all in vain.

So Monica tried a different strategy based on 1 Peter 3:1-2 (NKJV): *"Wives, likewise, be submissive to your own husbands, that even if some do not obey the word, they, without a word, may be won by the conduct of their wives,* ² *when they observe your chaste conduct accompanied by fear."*

She decided that more than words, her conduct could be the vehicle to Patricius's conversion. Because of this "strategy",

Monica led her own mother-in-law to Christ through her perseverance in meekness and patience.

Monica was known in the community as one who fervently prayed for her entirely family to come to know the Lord. She was also known as a great peacemaker because she helped settle many discords and helped heal disputes.

She did her best to raise her children in the ways of God, and it caused her much anguish when they strayed from God's truth.

Patricius and Monica had a son whom I'll name Gus (for now). He was a most promising son and was blessed with an exceptional education.

Monica thought that *this* education would be the means by which Gus would fully know GOD. But alas, it wasn't to be so.

Gus refused to heed the warnings of his mother, and instead plunged into a life of sexual immorality, lust and self-gratification. He even fathered a child while living with a woman who was *not* his wife.

But none of these things deterred Monica from fervently praying for both her husband and her son.

And like a good mother, Monica did not let Gus's foolishness, blatant sin and hard-heartedness obstruct or cloud her ***relentless love*** for him.

Regarding her husband, thankfully, in the final year before his death, Patricius converted to Christianity because of Monica's *consistent* prayers for him, and the godly conduct she exhibited toward him based on 1 Peter 3:1-2.

Monica's **relentless love** for her husband paid off in the end!

But her son Gus *still* wouldn't listen to any of Monica's words about Christianity. So from then on, her main strategy changed: instead of more talk about Christianity, her main mission was to solely and *fervently pray* for her son to turn to GOD.

Gus eventually moved to Rome to teach, and widowed Monica followed her son there. Later, he moved to Milan without telling his mother, and even then, Monica miraculously found out where her son was, and moved to Milan.

In Milan, she attended a church pastored by a man named Ambrose. Monica was delighted when Ambrose befriended Gus!

Because of Ambrose's friendship with Gus and the way the former explained some of the tenets of Christianity to the latter, Gus eventually became a Christian!

*Finally*, after 17 long years of Monica's fervent prayers for Gus, she lived to see him turn to Christ Jesus. This practically matched her long wait for her husband to become a Christian, because she had prayed for Patricius for 30 years!

Well, I called him Gus earlier. Let me now reveal Gus's full name: Augustine.

St. Augustine's ministry included his famous writings called "The Confessions" and his ministry would continue through the centuries to later influence Luther and Calvin.

Inside "The Confessions", Augustine reveals what his beloved mother Monica once said, *"There was only one reason, and one reason alone why I wished to remain a little longer in this life, and it was to see you become a Christian."*

Before she passed away at the age of 56, Monica enjoyed a deep spiritual friendship with her son Augustine. She died a fulfilled and happy woman knowing that her consistent, heartfelt prayers through all those years had been answered.

**The End**

This indeed is a true story of *relentless love* – Monica's relentless love for her husband and son.

May this encourage you to stay committed in your relentless prayers for a prodigal child you may know, or a wayward spouse.

Remember, you too can be RELENTLESS in *love*. "

My hope is that through the stories I shared in this chapter, you may become even *more* relentless in *faith*, relentless in *hope*, and relentless in *love*.

"And now these three remain: faith, hope and love. But the greatest of these is love." 1 Corinthians 13:13 NIV

*L→R: Alyssa, Jackie, Jim and Michael at their favorite coffee house – Social Grounds Coffee & Tea Co., which serves the best mochas in town, although not yet to their kids.*

# JACKIE LANSANGAN–MOREY

Jackie is a premier entrepreneur, 8-time #1 International Bestselling Author, Book Publisher, Editor, Virtual Book Launch Host/Consultant, and Prophetic Mentor.

She's also a WebTV Host and Producer of "Jackie Morey LIVE", "The 21st Century Legacy Letters", "The Exponential You", and is the Founder and CEO of Customer Strategy Academy.

Her passion is to help leaders, consultants, coaches, business professionals, medical professionals, writers and entrepreneurs – to grow their business & live their lives purposefully and by design, not by default, through her Book Writing, Editing, Book Publishing, and Online Marketing businesses.

As a degreed Engineer, she brings her unique logical expertise to simplify the nuts and bolts of writing, self-publishing and launching her clients to Bestselling Authors. Jackie is a recognized Revenue-Generator, Relationship Ambassador, Topnotch Solution Provider, Creative Problem-solver, Peacemaker, and Team-builder.

She enjoys movies, gourmet dark chocolate, traveling, jazz, pop and classical music, chess, writing, bike riding, volleyball, table tennis, having coffee with family and friends, savoring sweet, juicy Philippine mangoes, snorkeling in the tropical beaches of Coron, Palawan, and sharing prophetic words with and for family members, friends, and occasionally, with complete strangers as the Lord leads.

She's happily married and lives in a beautiful Pacific Northwest suburb of Seattle with her husband Jim. They have a son and a daughter who "make them proud" every day.

Connect with Jackie:

Facebook: www.facebook.com/JackieMorey77
LinkedIn: www.linkedin.com/in/jackiemorey1
Twitter: www.Twitter.com/JackieMorey1

## CHAPTER 8
# Further Down the Road
### By Billy A. San Juan

### WINNING WORDS

All my life, *words* have enamored me.

My mom taught me how to read when I was four years of age.

Yes, picture words. Dog. Cat. Cow. Box. Red. Green. Black and White.

I got to know names. David. Ann. John. Mary. Will and Puss.

If you recognize these names, good for you!

You see, these books were not mine. They were all hand-me-downs, although unused. These books were my sisters' Reading and Writing books.

I have two older sisters, Maria Victoria, who's older by two years. The first-born, Veronica Martha, is older by three. And as soon as my two sisters got their books for school, I asked my mother to read all of them to me. Well, at least the ones *with stories*.

At school, when others were out to play during recess time, I was *inside* the library combing an edition of The World Almanac or a volume of Encyclopedia Britannica.

Once a librarian even *shooed* me away because I strayed into a library section off-limits to grade-school students!

I joined spelling, essay-writing and declamation contests, not because I was an outstanding writer and speaker. But because I'd always cherished this kind of battle with **words**. I didn't always end up on top, but boy the thrill and joy I felt was *unmatched!*

I clearly remember a Spelling Bee contest when I was eight years old. It was the final round. Only two of us were left. The first speller, Medardo Macaraig, *didn't* spell his word correctly on the three attempts. If I got mine right, I would snatch the gold medal.

The word was LIAR.

I began spelling the word: L-I-E-R. Wrong, try again. L-I-E-R. Think. You spelled it wrong. On my final attempt, L-I-E-R. Sorry, you didn't get it!

Medardo proceeded to spell the word "BUSINESS" and I settled for the silver.

Was I crushed? Well, ah, not really…because I saw the beaming faces and proud looks from my father and mother as the silver medal was draped on my chest!

It was one of the happiest days of my life!

Looking back, I did not spell the word correctly because I *didn't* recognize the word. It was *not* in my vocabulary. We never used the expression because there was never any need for it in our family.

Truth was a virtue taught by my parents at home and by our teachers at school. And I am glad that at that early age, I was introduced to **honesty** and **integrity**. With these words, you are always a winner.

And I guess my daddy and mommy knew why I got a shining silver medal!

## PEDRO, JUNIOR

My daddy, Pedro Macandog San Juan, Jr., fondly called Junior by family and friends, was a hardworking and busy parent. He was a quiet and private person.

I never had lengthy conversations with him. I only remember two instances of an extended talk with "daddy."

The first, when I decided to take the entrance exam for the University of the Philippines (U.P.) High School enrolment. Yes, daddy let me choose which action to take, stay or move.

But before I made the decision, daddy patiently and clearly explained all the possible outcomes and consequences of my choice. If I stayed, I'd skip one grade level (7th) and go straight to Lourdes High as an accelerated student. If I took the test and passed, I'd get into UP High. Fail, and I'd return to Lourdes Grade School and take an extra year.

Letting me pick what school to choose was a sign of my dad's love and respect for his son. And I realized much later that it is a wise father who knows his own son, not willing for him to be lost, and instead, to give into his son's hands as much as he possibly could.

The other long exchange we had was some time in 1985.

I was seriously involved in the people's movement to oust then dictator, Ferdinand Marcos.

He came home one night, sat me down on the table, and told me that the son of his friend almost died. That son, let's call him Raul (for confidentiality), was also my "comrade" from U.P.

Dad narrated how Raul was arrested by the military, told to dig his grave and was about to be shot if not for some friendly general who intervened! He was freed and flown to another country immediately upon release.

He told me to take care of myself, but never asked me to stop doing the things I believed in.

Incidentally, my dad was a Marcos admirer. But I know that dad had no conflict, knowing that his son was walking in the truth.

I can still feel his hand wrapped on my 8-year-old hand, as we walked along Rizal Avenue in Sta. Cruz, Manila.

There I was, trying to match his long steps with my double steps. Seeking the best burgers and hotdogs in town. Buying hot "hopiang munggo" (a Chinese dessert) and browsing used books and magazines along book stalls.

I don't remember any of the words spoken, but I can still vividly recall all the thoughts shared.

Pedro, Jr. suffered from Parkinsonism and dementia in his later years. He died at the age of 72.

## BETTY

Let me tell you about my mother.

My mother, Beatriz Ricafrente Abarro, Betty for short, was a typical "barrio" (provincial small town) lass. She was born during the 1930s during the Great Depression, also called peacetime in Manila. She went to the barrio school in Bagbag – a small town in Rosario, Cavite.

Every day she walked to school, the village elders always teased her, "Pango, pango!" (flat-nosed, flat-nosed). The teasing became so intense that sometimes she had to take the much longer route to school.

But nothing could stop young Betty from completing her studies.

She had high ambitions. She planned to work in Manila when the opportunity allowed. Every day, she trudged to school over the rice fields and meadows of Bagbag.

Then the Japanese invaded the Philippines.

At nine years of age, she witnessed the bombing of the U.S. Naval Base in Sangley Point in Cavite City on December 8, 1942, just a few kilometers from their home!

My mom regrettably experienced the horrible atrocities of war.

She used to tell stories of how, as a little girl, she witnessed the Japanese soldiers **behead** suspected Filipino patriot-guerrillas!

She saw *"Makapili"* – pro-Japanese *Filipino traitors* who, with their heads covered with a "bayong" (a native bag woven with buri palm leaves) for secrecy – pointed out, identified, and betrayed anti-Japanese, Filipino patriot-town mates and neighbors for their immediate incarceration, torture and execution – in exchange for the promise of land, wealth and other resources to be distributed after the war.

She told us how our grandfather Honorio, whom we fondly called "Tata Eryong", quietly hid inside the ceiling when the Japanese marched into town.

Tata Eryong was a U.S. Navy band member. He kept a clarinet and a .38 caliber pistol in his "baul" (wooden chest). The music instrument he would allow me handle, the other one was ***off-limits***. I was four years old.

It was an exceedingly dark moment in our country's history.

Many of Tata Eryong's bandmates were captured and killed!

But thankfully, he and my mother endured, survived, and pulled through. I guess I inherited some of their *"tough stuff"* genes! Later in life, I would deal with similar conditions and had to respond with the same grit. But let's talk about this later.

In wartime, young girls and women were kept away in hiding, to elude sexual abuse and violence by the occupying forces. They had to hide in the rice fields to avoid the Japanese troops. My mom would spend almost all the years of wartime hidden from sight!

Isn't it funny that we find ourselves in the same situation today in the year 2020? Hiding from a virus inside our houses? Probably the reason why they call the pandemic "a war."

Life was difficult. Food was scarce.

I remember my mother telling us how a piece of pork or fish meat wafting on the surface of "ginisang munggo" (Mung Bean soup) was like heaven-on-earth. And this meager meal was rationed among her brothers and sisters – *seven in all*.

As with *all other* regular activities during peacetime, education and learning grounded to a complete halt; Betty's hopes for the higher scholarship disappeared.

But you see, Betty is hardy…and ***relentless***!

After the war, she finished her primary education. She recounted how her mother wept because they couldn't finance her nursing studies any further.

So she took up a secretarial course, and upon completion of her certification, began to hunt for work in Manila.

One day, my grandmother "Basilisa" – who had heard that there were openings at the phone company – asked if Betty was ready to work.

It was 1953, and with telephone subscribers outpacing the pre-war levels, the Philippine Long-Distance Telephone Company (PLDT) required new switchboard operators. No need for a college degree. The applicant would simply need to be willing and trainable.

My mother became part of the *first team* of telephone operators trained by PLDT *after* World War 2!

Her first office destination was called the Riverside Office. More accurately, it was in the Singson Building at Riverside Drive in Sta. Cruz, Manila. The office was on the street right behind the Manila Post Office beside the Pasig River, the major waterway bisecting Manila and the surrounding urban areas into northern and southern halves.

The 25 kilometer-long Pasig river connects Laguna de Bay to Manila Bay. It snakes through Manila, Makati, Mandaluyong, Pasig, Taguig, and Taytay in Rizal Province.

Riverside Drive still serves the traveling public today.

She rode a provincial bus daily, Saulog Transit or St. Raphael Bus Lines, to get from home to work and back. The trip would've taken *over two hours each way!*

I remember going to our hometown on a public bus back in the late 90s. It took an hour and thirty minutes on well-paved roads and highways, including the newly-opened Manila-Cavite Coastal Road.

In the 50s, the old Manila West Road or Highway 17 originated from Zapote, Las Pinas, and via a circuitous route, passed through Bacoor, Imus, and all the way to Silang, Cavite.

Every day, for *two hours* in the early morning and *two hours* in the early evening, she would be on a bus.

Alas, one can't miss the similarity with the present-day travails of the Filipino commuter.

Nevertheless, what made it bearable then was that the northern terminus of the provincial bus was in Plaza Lawton (now **Liwasang Bonifacio**, Manila) a few steps away…right in front of the *Manila Post Office*.

Little did I know that 30 years later, I would walk on the same asphalt road my mother used to tread…

## STUDENT MARCH

It was 1981, January 17, and President Ferdinand Marcos announced the *"lifting"* of Martial Law after nine *long* years. It was a strange declaration.

The President proclaimed the New Republic, yet Marcos retained all presidential decrees, legislative powers, *and* the privilege of the writ of habeas corpus was *still suspended!*

These were the reasons why many called it a *fake lifting*, an old dog with a new collar.

Together with workers, students, the urban poor, priests, and nuns – a few prominent politicians held a big rally in **Liwasang Bonifacio**. The group called for the dismantling of the US-supported Marcos regime.

They also called for a boycott of the scheduled Presidential elections in June of the same year. And yes, I was there, in front of the **Manila Post Office**.

The "fake lifting" came at the heels of an awakened student movement that fought to restore students' rights and welfare, a movement banned during the dark episode of martial rule.

One by one, we regained student councils and restored campus publications.

The student gains were the beginning of the long walk back to freedom.

I was both witness and participant in history.

I remember going home once from the U.P. High School in 1977, riding a public bus, passing a mass of students through the main university campus gates.

They were thumping the wooden body of our bus, shouting, "Council ibalik!" meaning "Restore the (Student) Council!"

My heart raced, not of fear but of agitation.

Here we were, in the middle of martial law. And these young students, barely two years my senior, were on the streets, fighting for their self-proclaimed rights?! Where did they get their *courage*, knowing that, during that time of Martial Law, the authorities could quickly throw them in in jail *without* a warrant?

Well, two years later, in 1979, I was *with them* marching when I entered University for my college studies

"Restore the Student Council! Recognize our Student Organizations! Kalayaan Ipaglaban! Demokrasya Ipaglaban!" – Fight for Freedom! Fight for Democracy!

*This* time, I knew where I drew my courage from. To borrow the words of the stoic Roman philosopher, Seneca the Younger, "He who is brave is free."

We marched around campus. We marched on the streets. We marched towards the Batasang Pambansa (National Legislative).

Yes, the police blocked our path. Yet the regime did *not* defeat us, and we restored the University Student Council (USC). The Philippine Collegian – our university newspaper re-emerged!

On September 5, 1980, the University held its first USC elections since 1973. Malou Mangahas became the first female Chairperson of the USC. She was also the Editor-in-Chief of the Philippine Collegian, the U.P. campus paper.

Six years later, on February 25, 1986, the people booted out President Marcos. We, the brave were **finally free!!**

## BACK TO BETTY...

Betty began her career in the telephone company. It proved to be a long and productive profession. Spanning 45 years, she was, you could say, someone who rose from the ranks.

She started as a switchboard operator and retired as a Senior Supervisor in the company! It was the highest position reserved for someone who did *not* have a college education.

She was still rank-and-file staff.

But as a Senior Supervisor, she earned much more than younger managers and vice presidents of the company! The company even provided her with an executive car. Not because of seniority – because others were with the company longer. She earned all of these perks through her *dedication* and *loyalty* to her work and company.

She was not merely a supervisor...she was also a confidant, a coach, and a friend. She was known as *"BSJ"*, even before initials became the moniker among executives in the corporate world.

I remember her having long conversations on the phone with colleagues and subordinates. I used to get annoyed when she hogged the phone line for extended lengths of time every night.

You see, this was the era when there was only *one* phone line per household. If you were unlucky, you would even share this with a neighbor, called a "party line."

It was much later that I realized *this* was her way of leading her people. She was shaping, instructing, and influencing them not only in work areas but, more importantly, their attitudes in life.

She did all of this voluntarily, beyond her work hours, not because her boss required it of her, but because she *genuinely* believed in investing into people.

I read the concept later from the works of modern-day success authors. Well, it was a principle shared and demonstrated to me by my mother every night, decades ago.

It was a well-taught lesson – the habit of making deposits into the emotional bank accounts of people you meet!

## CLARK

It was July 2008, and I had to make a crucial decision.

I was the Head Executive Assistant for the **Clark Freeport Zone** President, **Levy P. Laus**. Employees and colleagues fondly called him **"LPL"**. For several years, I worked as a consultant for the companies he owned – the Laus Group of Companies or LGC. The rising countryside tycoon operated the largest multi-brand car dealership north of Manila.

LPL engaged me in helping organize the local business chamber. Having incorporated the Pampanga Chamber of

Commerce and Industry or PAMCHAM, LPL invited me to join the LGC as his Executive Assistant for External Affairs.

It began a long relationship with LPL spanning almost 17 years.

We had a mentor-mentee relationship. LPL, a stern taskmaster, demanded details in the planning and excellence in the execution.

Frequently he would tell me, *"I am not asking you to be perfect. I am asking you to be ideal."*

On the surface, I was clueless about how to differentiate perfection from *the ideal*. When LPL first said this line, I told myself that he probably couldn't find the exact word.

But, as time passed, I slowly grasped the essence of this enigmatic message.

You see, many times, I was criticized, warned, and rebuked by LPL for numerous slipups, errors, and blunders in my work. When you worked for the company owner, you knew that your hold was never permanent nor secure, meaning that the owner had the power to fire you on the spot at any given time.

There was an occasion when I failed to answer a call from LPL while driving along the North Luzon Express Way. It was a short 20-minute drive, so I decided to return the call after I reached my destination. I didn't know that the chairman needed details, which I held, on a contract that he was negotiating over the phone.

He scolded me personally when I arrived at the office. The company almost lost a considerable amount of money because of my decision not to stop at several parking bays along the way to answer his call.

I learned *then* how to respect the value of executive time!

On another occasion, I accepted a Christmas gift on behalf of LPL from a Korean business partner. I *didn't* list down the items I received.

Little did I know that these were very expensive Ginseng roots worth *tens of thousands in pesos!*

The rebuke that followed was *brutal*. He told me *not* to take, much less touch any of the presents that I had personally stowed inside his private office.

I was downcast. Never did it cross my mind to take something that wasn't mine! I had never exhibited any signs of deceitfulness in any of my official dealings within the company.

But the censure was right. I knew that LPL didn't have any idea of what was given and what was received. He only had *my word*.

Trust has to be earned by giving a proper accounting of your actions, in *all* things, whether big or small!

## RUNNING STRONG

The **Clark Freeport and Special Economic Zone** is a business, industry, aviation, education, and tourism hub located in the rapidly-growing province of Pampanga, Philippines. It has an international airport, a National Government Center, sports, gaming, and leisure facilities to cater to the Central Luzon populace.

It has numerous outdoor greens. The Bicentennial Park, Picnic Grounds, El Kabayo Ranch, and the Clark Parade Grounds. It had ideal places where you could clear your mind and enjoy the fresh air while working up a sweat as you kept fit.

A Prussian philosopher once said, *"True enjoyment comes from activity of the mind and exercise of the body; the two are ever united."*

This atmosphere set the stage for one of the most unbelievable points in my life.

I call it *my running years*.

When LPL accepted the position two years prior, in October 2006 to head the Clark Development Corporation, he brought only two persons. His driver, Wilfran Esteban, and me, as his Executive Assistant.

Some pretty good perks came along with the position. My family stayed in a three-bedroom villa located inside the free port – fully furnished, with free electricity, a lovely terrace, and centralized air-conditioning. Clark provided me with an executive vehicle, free gasoline, with a personal driver to boot!

All along, I thought pleasures and comforts comprised *"living the good life"*.

What I didn't know was slowly, I was turning into a fat slob.

Well, to be kinder to myself, I'll call myself an *alimentive* person. Cheerful. Optimistic. Easy-going. But physically round-bellied, slow-moving, and with a waddle-like walk. Oh, and *did I say fat?*

To be fair, I wasn't always a heavyweight.

Years earlier, I was a high-school athlete…a slim teen (look at my yearbook photos) who ran every afternoon with a small group of school mates – who equally loved running.

My running buddies were Chally Romero, brothers John and Paul Encarnacion, brothers Leonid and Fidel Nemenzo, Edwin Peralta, and Michael Keon from the U.P. Road Runners Club.

Our small group joined large and small track meets, long and short road races, and mountain trail runs in U.P. Los Baños. We would run inside the exclusive subdivisions of Quezon City and on the hills of Capitol and Monte Vista. It was so enjoyable that afternoon runs turned into night runs at the finish.

But like other high school pursuits, running had to give way to new interests, hobbies, and friends.

I know John continues to run to this day. He is now a certified finisher of the Boston Marathon, the Crème de la crème of all marathons world-wide.

When I entered the University of the Philippines, the raging student movement absorbed much of my time. After the 1986 EDSA People's Revolution, I joined the corporate world, became a financial wiz, and by the age of 40, had married my wife Marian and were blessed with a sweet daughter, Pace Christiane.

I was also ready to get out of the rat race and launch a startup in Pampanga.

I ended up eventually working in Clark for LPL. And *did I say became fat?*

But I am *relentless*, right?

The perfect ambiance of Clark Freeport Zone set the stage for my running comeback.

Well, candidly, it's walking.

From my running weight of 125 lbs. in high school, I ballooned into a 190-lb. gentle panda. Running would have permanently damaged my knees. I was content with my afternoon stroll along the path around the Clark Parade Grounds.

But an exciting event was fast-approaching Clark in the early days of January 2008. Two Kenyan runners, the gods of running – were racing for the first time on Philippine soil. And it was to take place in Clark!

To represent the President of the Clark Development Corporation or CDC, I had to meet and greet the Kenyan runners. Two Kenyan runners arrived shortly before sunset of Friday, two days before the January 13 Clark Freeport International Marathon race.

The visitors flew in through Clark International Airport and headed towards the CDC offices. I expected a short photo session with the Kenyan runners and then I'd head to my dinner date shortly thereafter.

But as soon as the Kenyans set foot on the parade grounds, they stripped off their tracksuits and, wearing just their running shorts and tees, proceeded to *run*!

*Did I say run?*

No, it was more of a *graceful lope,* like gazelles galloping with their feet floating above the ground.

Beside me was the Philippine Marathon champion Sgt. Eduardo *"Vertek"* Buenavista to greet the Kenyans. But not to be outdone, he donned his racing shorts and ran with the visiting Kenyans!

They called it a shakedown run before the 42.195-kilometer race. A final test to see if the runners' legs were ready.

I thought it would just be a couple of laps around the 2.2-kilometer parade ground perimeter, and we'd call it a night.

On the fifth lap, Vertek ended his run.

The Kenyans continued to go around *five* more times

around before finally stopping. An incredible 22-kilometer tune-up *two* days before the big race.

I stood there the entire 1 hour and 30 minutes watching these super humans doing a 4-minute kilometer pace around and around.

Amazing!

Right then and there, I told myself that I would run a marathon.

It would help me lose some weight and be as impressive as the Kenyan runners.

Well, Saturday morning, I overslept. Too tired from standing around, gaping at the runners, I asked myself, "Am I to doomed to wear Size 40 pants all my life?"

Sunday, race day. I had to get up early – at 4:00 am – to accompany LPL, who would fire the starting gun.

The race was on, and guess who won the race? Right. Hilary Lagat, the first Kenyan marathoner to race in the Philippines in 2 hours, 26 minutes and 29 seconds!

Nothing could stop me now from my first marathon after that. I was committed!

At first, baby steps. My walk-jog-walk became a walk-run-walk, then turned into a jog-run-jog. Finally this became a **run-run-run**!

After three months, I could continuously run one lap around the parade grounds. A full marathon was 19 laps around.

I mentally counted how long it would take before I was ready: Four years, nine months, and eight days! What?! I wanted to *run from running*!

There is a profound life lesson I learned from running, and that is: **Progress is not linear.**

There would be great days and weeks ahead. But there would be down moments as well.

The important thing is *to have faith in the plan and to stick to it*.

When one commits to this, soon, they'll realize that weakness and pain do build *strength* and *endurance*.

You *can* recover from the aches that will enable you to come back – and come back *stronger*, reinforcing each fiber of the your *physical*, *mental*, and *spiritual* capacities.

No, it didn't take me four years to run my first marathon.

On October 24, 2009, at 5:30 pm, I toed the starting line 42.195 kilometers away from the Subic Bay Special Economic Zone finishing chute at Remy Field Stadium.

With my proud daughter and wife watching, I set off to the first of tens of thousands of strides of my marathon career.

I was a back of the pack runner. This now 155-lb person may not be as lightning-quick as the Kenyan gods, but he sure is a finisher.

And he might have taken over five hours to finish a marathon, but he does have *five marathon finisher medals* on his chest!

I continued to run minor races after my last 42K in 2013.

Well, I was beginning a new marathon training cycle for a 2014 race when I felt a tinge of pain on my right knee. It was the first sign of osteoarthritis. It was distressing at first. I was in denial.

I tried herbal treatments and strengthening supplements. I didn't want to stop. My doctor told me to take it easy. Sadly, I asked him if I could do the marathon one last time. He said, "Yes."

And I am reserving that *one last marathon* for when I'm 60 years old.

## BACK TO WORDS

In July of 2008, LPL decided to relinquish his post as President & CEO.

First, a disclosure.

I knew all along that my stint in Clark wasn't going to be a permanent thing. Sooner or later, I would have to give up my privileges. But then again, LPL is both faithful and big-hearted.

He gave me two choices. The opportunity to stay at Clark, choose whatever position I wished, retain all the benefits, and in a permanent capacity.

The other pick was I would work for him at one of his other companies. For me, it was an easy choice.

On August 31, 2008, I joined his newly-built television station, the first free TV station outside Metro Manila, CLTV36.

It was a daunting task to operate a television station well outside its center of business and industry. But we were blessed with brave and innovative teams that helped transform a once-devastated province into a metropolitan and progressive haven. (Note: The Mt. Pinatubo eruption in 1991 almost buried the entire province of Pampanga in volcanic ash.)

The media industry has converted Pampanga into an attractive locus for commerce and trade, formerly monopolized by and concentrated in Metro Manila. All we had to do is portray our people's strength and grit, and the investments began to pour in.

On April 25, 2019, we lost LPL. He died in a helicopter crash over the fields of Central Luzon. His vision of countryside development remains alive.

And as with any story, it all comes full circle.

Words.

**Stories** are comprised of *words*.

I've always been enamored by **stories**.

Whether sharing life lessons, encouraging others, or motivating myself, *words* have been essential in my lifelong journey on this earth.

An Australian-German writer, Marcus Zusak, wrote, *"The best word shakers were the ones who understood the true power of words. They were the ones who could climb the highest."*

I continue to strive toward a **higher purpose**, just like Pedro, Jr. who shaped my heart. Just like Betty continues to do at the age of 87. And just as LPL did before his untimely death.

And whether one succeeds or not, let us keep on *telling our stories* so that others can pick up where we let off.

You see, success is on the same road as failure, success is just a little further down the road.

L ➔R: *Daughter Pace, Wife Marian, and Billy*

## Billy A. San Juan

Billy was born Virgilio Hernando Abarro San Juan to Pedro Jr. and Beatriz. He grew up and lived in Manila, Philippines, for 39 years.

He graduated from the University of the Philippines (U.P.) with a Bachelor of Science in Community Development.

He is a proponent of active citizenship, having helped empower informal settlers around the U.P. communities, organize youth organizations, assist start-up entrepreneurs and family businesses, and restore the livelihood of fisherfolks in Daang Bantayan affected by Typhoon Haiyan.

He has prior professional involvement in Leader Imports, All Asia Capital Resources, International Netherlands Group, and the Philippine Business for Social Progress. He is now the Vice President of Central Luzon TV36, the country's only regional free television channel operating outside Metro Manila. He is currently the managing Officer-in-Charge of SunStar Pampanga, a local newspaper and an affiliate of SunStar Philippines.

Billy is married to Marian de Jesus, and the Lord blessed them with a daughter, Pace Christiane. They now live in Apalit, Pampanga.

## CHAPTER 9

# The Character of Relentless Leaders

By Rev. Dante Eleazar "Bong" Simon

The word "RELENTLESS" is dictionary-defined as – showing or promising no abatement of severity, intensity, strength, or pace. It also means: UNRELENTING, relentless pressure such as a relentless campaign

Some synonyms are: determined, dogged, implacable, unappeasable, unflinching.

So what are the characteristics of a relentless leader?

### Words from the experts he interviewed....

I've been able to glean wisdom from Deep Patel's bestselling book "A Paperboy's Fable: The 11 Principles of Success". Patel interviewed several CEOs, professors, entrepreneurs, and General David Petraeus, and I'd like to share some of my takeaways from his book with you.

Every path to success starts with a vision; it's what gives you direction. It's your reason for working as hard as you do. Once you have a vision for what you want your future to look like, you need to set a series of goals to achieve this dream – this is your plan for getting there.

Your vision is your mission and should be something you have clearly defined and written down. It's a chance to put your thoughts, ideas, and values into action. It's also the benchmark you can use to chart your progress, to see how far you've come and remind yourself where you're going.

You have to believe that you have what it takes. Mental challenges will be among the biggest obstacles you face – the kind that make you question yourself and what you're doing. Without a healthy dose of self-confidence, you'll be tempted to accept defeat when you should be finding a way to bounce back from failure.

**Here are some questions I would like you to think about...**

What have you been given? What are your talents, abilities , gifts, experiences, and skills?

Many times God works with what is already in *your* hand. What is in *your* hand?

What can you do?

## They take action

Unstoppable people don't wait until they feel "secure" before making big leaps. They jump in and keep going!

From that first push to get the ball rolling, to those decisive moments when you must correct your course, **action** is fundamental to success.

Making big decisions and taking leaps of faith can be both terrifying and exciting. It's your chance to think big and be bold.

Sometimes *inaction* is hidden behind other issues, such as poor time management and lack of self-discipline.

Stop waiting and stop making excuses. If you want to be **relentless**, put your energy into action *now*. Fail to do so and your vision will sit on a shelf, gathering dust.

Those who are relentless don't allow themselves to be thwarted by change. They understand they must be resilient and versatile, or risk becoming ineffective and irrelevant.

You either learn to bend and flex or you will be broken and discarded.

Relentless leaders are fully committed to their goals.

Are you letting life happen to you, *or* are you shaping your life through the power of sheer will and hard work?

Unstoppable people develop habits that keep them focused and they cultivate an insatiable hunger to go after their dreams.

Consider some Powerful Questions from American author, speaker, and pastor – John Maxwell regarding *different* kinds of decisions:

*Courageous decisions* – What must be done?
*Priority decisions* – What must be done first?
*Change decisions* – What must be done differently?
*Creative decisions* – What might be possible?

## They persist through life's storms

You can be the most talented, intelligent, and creative person out there, but without persistence you are doomed to mediocrity at best.

Successful and unstoppable people know they must dig deep and find their *grit* if they're to reach their goals. They don't let hurdles hold them back; instead, they find a way around obstacles to keep moving forward.

Persistence is a habit as well as a character trait that you must develop to get you through tough times and to keep procrastination from getting the best of you.

Long-term dreams are a labor of love. Day in and day out, you must reject discouragement and remain focused on your objectives.

## They are self-aware

***"Know thyself"*** is a well-known Ancient Greek aphorism quoted by several Greek philosophers such as Socrates and Plato. Knowing ourselves and becoming self-aware allows us to understand ourselves as unique individuals, beyond the roles we play with friends and family or in society.

Being self-aware means understanding who you are *underneath it all*: your patterns of behavior, know yourself, know your strengths and weaknesses.

Good thinkers solve problems, they never lack ideas for building an organization, and they always have hope for a better future.

I've studied successful people for forty years, and though the diversity you find among them is astounding, I've found that they are all alike in one way: **how they think!** This is the *one thing* that separates successful people from unsuccessful ones.

And here's the good news. How successful people think, *can* be learned. If you change your thinking, you can change your life!

Unstoppable people have an internal drive that propels them to success. They are intrinsically motivated, meaning they have a deep internal desire or impulse to pursue their goals. You see, when motivation **comes from within**, it tends to be more meaningful – you feel compelled to keep moving forward, even if there is no external reward.

*Extrinsic motivation*, on the other hand, is usually based on an external reward of some kind. You decide to take a new job because it offers better compensation. But the allure of external incentives subsides over time. Those who are truly driven and unstoppable aren't doing it for the fat salary or benefits packages – they are doing it because they feel they *must*.

## They take responsibility

Taking responsibility has two parts: You answer for your mistakes and failures, but you also take credit for your successes. Relentless people *own* their failures as much as they *revel* in their accomplishments.

They acknowledge and learn from *both* failures and successes, in order to gain the wisdom and knowledge necessary to pursue even bigger dreams and goals.

Taking responsibility is about acknowledging that you, and you alone, are in charge of your life. You're in the driver's seat, and no one else can dictate your future.

## They surround themselves with other high achievers

Relationships are an important part of life because we often reflect the attitudes and behaviors of those, we spend time with. Spend too much time with negative people and you may find yourself drifting into a pessimistic mindset.

Successful and unstoppable people surround themselves with good company. They gravitate toward other go-getters.

Look for others who inspire you and whose insights open your mind to new possibilities. You'll discover that they are voracious learners.

Our ability to *learn* and *grow* is key to our ability to *improve* and *innovate*. To be unstoppable, you must embrace learning. You should be an avid consumer of information and be constantly seeking to educate yourself.

Becoming a voracious learner feeds your mind by allowing new connections and ideas to flourish. Those who relentlessly pursue their goals never stop seeking to expand their understanding and increase their knowledge of the world around them.

Allow me to give you some examples of high achievers:

**Bener Agtarap, PhD** – Asst Gensec Executive Director Path 1 UMC, The General Board of Discipleship

**Rowena Arrieta** – World-class pianist. She is the only Filipina who studied at the famous Tchaikovsky School of Music in Moscow, The Soviet Union

**Lemuel Balagot** – Filipino entrepreneur, owner of L.A. Rose, the longest running Filipino restaurant in Los Angeles. He is proudly Filipino. Lemuel is also my uncle.

**Anton Boisen** – Dr. and Founder of Clinical Pastoral Education

**Warner Brown** – United Methodist Bishop, and President of the Council of Bishops, The United Methodist Church

**Silvanetto Benoni, PhD** – Filipino Methodist pastor, Educator, Author, Psychotherapist

**Attorney Noelle Riza Castillo** – Legal Counsel, Partner at Castillo, De Luna, Abueg, Castro Lawyers, Church leader

## They are never fully satisfied

Relentless and persistent people are never fully satisfied with their achievements. They feel compelled to keep pressing on, to keep looking for the next big thing. They don't allow themselves to slack off or rest on the laurels of their past accomplishments.

Unstoppable people are always in pursuit. They stay focused on the next challenge and continue pushing toward the next level of excellence.

## They develop mental resilience

With ambition comes mental pressure, and sometimes *that* stress is a heavy burden. Many people crumble under stress, consumed by anxiety and tension. Therefore, to become unstoppable, you must develop the mental fortitude to handle adversity and failure.

Developing *mental toughness* will keep you strong, determined, and focused during the rocky times, and will help keep your emotions in check when you need to be strong.

Unrelenting people don't run from adversity. They realize that facing a stressful situation head-on is a chance to prove that they can overcome and excel under duress!

*Mental fortitude* is the voice that tells you: "Life is tough, but **you** are tougher!"

Here are some examples of those with mental resilience:

**Emerito Nacpil, PhD** – from Drew University, Filipino theologian, Filipino United Methodist Bishop

**Jackie Lansangan Morey** – Entrepreneur, Publisher, Life Coach.

**Cecilio Lorenzana** – Filipino Protestant Bishop, Co-Founder of The United Church of Christ in the Philippines

**Evelyn Mandac** – World-class Soprano, trained at the University of the Philippines and the world-renowned Julliard School of Music

**Michael Jordan** – World-class basketball player, perhaps the greatest player that ever played the sport

**John Maxwell** – Pastor, Speaker, Bestselling author on leadership and successful living

**John and Charles Wesley** – Preachers and Revivalists in England

There is a huge difference between self-confidence and ego.

Self-confidence is when you understand your worth and believe in yourself. Ego is when your sense of self becomes overly inflated and you become focused on self-interest. Ego and arrogance are often closely related to jealousy and resentment.

Unstoppable leaders understand that ego and jealousy operate out of fear. They recognize that, if left unchecked, these emotions will get in the way of their own success. Conversely, humility will bring out the best in those around you.

Pride and resentment are a waste of time and energy. Someone else's success is not a threat to your own advancement; their achievements don't spell your failure. Ditch the defensiveness and stop making it all about you.

To be unstoppable, focus on results and keep your mind on the goal.

*"Just as the yin-yang symbol possesses a kernel of light in the dark, and of dark in the light, creative leaps are grounded in a technical foundation."* — Josh Waitzkin, author of "The Art of Learning: An Inner Journey to Optimal Performance"

Become a master of your craft.

While everyone else is relaxing, you're practicing and perfecting. Learn the left-brained rules in and out, so that your right brain can have limitless freedom to "break the rules" and **create**.

With enhanced consciousness, time will slow down for you. You'll see things in several *more* frames than others. While they're trying to react to the situation, you'll be able to manipulate and tweak the situation to your liking!

Most people are competing with other people. They continuously check-in to see what others in their space (their "competition") are doing. As a result, they mimic and copy what's "working."

Conversely, when you create, you'll leave your competition behind. Competing with others makes absolutely *zero sense* to you. Why? Because it pulls you from your **authentic zone**.

So you must *zone-out* all the external noise and instead zone-in, through your *intrinsic motivation* and zone-in to your *authentic zone*, so that you can produce.

## They never stop learning

Ordinary people seek entertainment. Extraordinary people seek education and learning.

When you want to become the best at what you do, you must never stop learning. Never stop improving and honing your skills and knowledge. Your unparalleled preparation is what gives you power. No one else is willing to pay the price you've paid.

John Maxwell summarizes the way relentless leaders think: *"They see the wisdom of big picture thinking."*

Here are some examples of leaders who never stop learning

**Ben Cabrera** aka Bencab – National Artist for Art, Painter sculptor *par excellence*

**Felicisimo Cao, PhD** – Executive Director, Young and Young Adult and Camping Ministries, Cal Nevada UMC Conference

**Camilo Osias** – Filipino statesman, one of the first "pensionados" (full-ride student scholars) from the Philippines to study in the United States, High Commissioner to the U.S. Congress, educator, author of Philippine Reader, Philippine Senate President, Author of "The Story of a Long Career of Varied Tasks." Camilo is my grandfather. I respectfully call him Lolo Camilo. (Lolo is Filipino for Grandfather)

**Nathanael Arnel De Pano** – OPM (Original Pilpino Music) Composer, arranger, choral conductor, producer, Filipino praise songs and cantatas

**Leni Hufana-Del Prado** – Christian believer, beauty pageant runner-up, model, actress, Christian worker, Bestselling Author

**Jose Maria Fleras** – Author of Bulwagang Gantimpala's longest-running plays "Noli Me Tangmere" and "El Filibusterismo". (These are adaptations of Philippine National Hero – Jose Rizal's novels with the same titles. Writer, playwright, Director of CEO of Rise Against Hunger, and on a personal note, one of my best friends.

**Paul Locke Granadosin** – Bishop, The United Methodist Church. He holds longest position in Episcopalian leadership in the Philippines.

## They always work on their mental strength

The better you can handle difficult and challenging situations under pressure, the further you'll go than others around you. Because they'll likely crumble under pressure.

The best training you will ever do is mental training. Wherever your mind goes, your body follows. Wherever your thoughts go, your life follows.

Confidence is one of your greatest assets.

You've heard it before: "Running a marathon is far more *mental* than physical." A person's ability to run a marathon—or do anything hard—is more a reflection of their level of confidence than their actual ability.

Surround yourself with people who remind you of the future, not the past.

## Relentless people reinvent themselves

**Elzar "Dodjie" Simon** – my brother, is an Industrial Engineer from the pioneer University of the Philippines. He was a multi-awarded employee at the Veterans Administration.

He went on to become CIO at the AIT and then worked in Sydney, Australia. After this, he worked at Port Elizabeth, moved to Wall Street at AIG, and now works with New York University (NYU) in New York, New York.

My brother never held an instrument before age 11 or 12. We only had a transistor radio that we listened to A.M. programs.

Elzar would later evolved as one of the best Original Pilipino Music Composer, garnering *all* major music awards including the Asia Song Fest Grand Prize, Metro Pop etc.

He then transitioned and reinvented himself as an international bestselling author of A.I. Hacked and A.I. 2 Reimagining the Future. He is a much sought out speaker and lecturer even as far as Harvard University.

He has been awarded by University of the Philippines (U.P.) College of Engineering as a Notable Alumnus and holds a Professorial chair in Artificial Intelligence at U.P.

## Biblical Verses to Inspire us to Be Relentless

I'd like to inspire you to become "RELENTLESS" by citing specific verses from the Word of God. I invite you to meditate on these ancient Scriptures.

Philippians 4:13 – I can do all things through him who strengthens me.

Isaiah 41:10 – Fear not, for I am with you; be not dismayed, for I am your God; I will strengthen you, I will help you, I will uphold you with my righteous right hand.

Deuteronomy 31:6 – Be strong and courageous. Do not fear or be in dread of them, for it is the Lord your God who goes with you. He will not leave you or forsake you.

Isaiah 40:31 – But they who wait for the Lord shall renew their strength; they shall mount up with wings like eagles; they shall run and not be weary; they shall walk and not faint.

1 Corinthians 10:13 – No temptation has overtaken you that is not common to man. God is faithful, and he will not let you be tempted beyond your ability, but with the temptation he will also provide the way of escape, that you may be able to endure it.

Exodus 15:2 – The Lord is my strength and my song, and he has become my salvation; this is my God, and I will praise him, my father's God, and I will exalt him.

Ephesians 6:10 – Finally, be strong in the Lord and in the strength of his might.

Deuteronomy 20:4 – For the Lord your God is he who goes with you to fight for you against your enemies, to give you the victory.

2 Corinthians 12:9-10 – But He said to me, 'My grace is sufficient for you, for my power is made perfect in weakness.' Therefore I will boast all the more gladly of my weaknesses, so that the power of Christ may rest upon me. For the sake of Christ, then, I am content with weaknesses, insults, hardships, persecutions, and calamities. For when I am weak, then I am strong.

Joshua 1:9 – Have I not commanded you? Be strong and courageous. Do not be frightened, and do not be dismayed, for the Lord your God is with you wherever you go.

2 Timothy 1:7 – For God gave us a spirit not of fear but of power and love and self-control.

Isaiah 12:2 – Behold, God is my salvation; I will trust, and will not be afraid; for the Lord God is my strength and my song, and he has become my salvation.

Matthew 11:28 – Come to me, all who labor and are heavy laden, and I will give you rest.

Isaiah 40:29 – He gives power to the faint, and to him who has no might he increases strength.

Psalm 27:1 – The Lord is my light and my salvation; whom shall, I fear? The Lord is the stronghold of my life; of whom shall I be afraid?

Psalm 31:24 – Be strong, and let your heart take courage, all you who wait for the Lord!

Psalm 73:26 – My flesh and my heart may fail, but God is the strength of my heart and my portion forever.

2 Corinthians 12:9 – But he said to me, 'My grace is sufficient for you, for my power is made perfect in weakness.' Therefore I will boast all the more gladly of my weaknesses, so that the power of Christ may rest upon me.

Mark 12:30 – And you shall love the Lord your God with all your heart and with all your soul and with all your mind and with all your strength.

Nehemiah 8:10 – Then he said to them, 'Go your way. Eat the fat and drink sweet wine and send portions to anyone who has nothing ready, for this day is holy to our Lord. And do not be grieved, for the joy of the Lord is your strength.'

Psalm 46:1 – God is our refuge and strength, a very present help in trouble.

Habakkuk 3:19 – God, the Lord, is my strength; He makes my feet like the deer's, He makes me tread on my high places.

Psalm 29:11 – May the Lord give strength to his people! May the Lord bless his people with peace.

John 16:33 – I have said these things to you, that in me you may have peace. In the world you will have tribulation. But take heart; I have overcome the world.

1 Peter 4:11 – Whoever speaks, as one who speaks oracles of God; whoever serves, as one who serves by the strength that God supplies—in order that in everything God may be glorified through Jesus Christ. To him belong glory and dominion forever and ever. Amen.

Matthew 6:33 – But seek first the kingdom of God and his righteousness, and all these things will be added to you.

Psalm 23:4 – Even though I walk through the valley of the shadow of death, I will fear no evil, for you are with me; your rod and your staff, they comfort me.

2 Timothy 4:17 – But the Lord stood by me and strengthened me, so that through me the message might be

fully proclaimed, and all the Gentiles might hear it. So I was rescued from the lion's mouth.

Psalm 118:14 – The Lord is my strength and my song; he has become my salvation.

2 Thessalonians 3:3 – But the Lord is faithful. He will establish you and guard you against the evil one.

1 Corinthians 13:4-8 – Love is patient and kind; love does not envy or boast; it is not arrogant or rude. It does not insist on its own way; it is not irritable or resentful; it does not rejoice at wrongdoing but rejoices with the truth. Love bears all things, believes all things, hopes all things, endures all things. Love never ends. As for prophecies, they will pass away; as for tongues, they will cease; as for knowledge, it will pass away.

1 Corinthians 16:14 – Let all that you do be done in love.

1 John 4:8 – Anyone who does not love does not know God, because God is love.

John 3:16 – For God so loved the world, that he gave his only Son, that whoever believes in him should not perish but have eternal life.

John 13:34-35 – A new commandment I give to you, that you love one another: just as I have loved you, you also are to love one another. By this all people will know that you are my disciples if you have love for one another.

Colossians 3:14 – And above all these put-on loves, which binds everything together in perfect harmony.

1 Peter 4:8 – Above all, keep loving one another earnestly, since love covers a multitude of sins.

John 15:13 – Greater love has no one than this, that someone lay down his life for his friends.

Mark 12:29-31 – Jesus answered, "The most important is, 'Hear, O Israel: The Lord our God, the Lord is one. And you shall love the Lord your God with all your heart and with all your soul and with all your mind and with all your strength.' The second is this: 'You shall love your neighbor as yourself.' There is no other commandment greater than these.

1 Corinthians 13:13 – So now faith, hope, and love abide, these three; but the greatest of these is love.

Ephesians 4:2 – …with all humility and gentleness, with patience, bearing with one another in love…

Proverbs 17:17 – A friend loves at all times, and a brother is born for adversity.

Romans 12:9 – Let love be genuine. Abhor what is evil; hold fast to what is good.

1 John 4:16 – So we have come to know and to believe the love that God has for us. God is love, and whoever abides in love abides in God, and God abides in him.

Luke 6:35 – But love your enemies, and do good, and lend, expecting nothing in return, and your reward will be great, and you will be sons of the Most High, for he is kind to the ungrateful and the evil.

1 John 3:1 – See what kind of love the Father has given to us, that we should be called children of God; and so we are. The reason why the world does not know us is that it did not know him.

1 Corinthians 13:4-7 – Love is patient and kind; love does not envy or boast; it is not arrogant or rude. It does not insist on its own way; it is not irritable or resentful; it does not rejoice at wrongdoing but rejoices with the truth. Love bears all things, believes all things, hopes all things, endures all things.

Romans 13:8 – Owe no one anything, except to love each other, for the one who loves another has fulfilled the law.

Romans 12:10 – Love one another with brotherly affection. Outdo one another in showing honor.

Ephesians 4:32 (ESV) – Be kind to one another, tenderhearted, forgiving one another, as God in Christ forgave you.

1 Thessalonians 5:16-22 (ESV) – Rejoice always, pray without ceasing, give thanks in all circumstances; for this is the will of God in Christ Jesus for you. Do not quench the Spirit. Do not despise prophecies...

Galatians 2:20 (ESV) – I have been crucified with Christ. It is no longer I who live, but Christ who lives in me. And the life I now live in the flesh I live by faith in the Son of God, who loved me and gave Himself for me.

John 3:16 (ESV) – For God so loved the world, that he gave

his only Son, that whoever believes in him should not perish but have eternal life.

Jeremiah 32:19 (ESV) – Great in counsel and mighty indeed, whose eyes are open to all the ways of the children of man, rewarding each one according to his ways and according to the fruit of his deeds.

Ephesians 2:8-9 (ESV) – For by grace you have been saved through faith. And this is not your own doing; it is the gift of God, not a result of works, so that no one may boast.

1 John 4:18 (ESV) – There is no fear in love, but perfect love casts out fear. For fear has to do with punishment, and whoever fears has not been perfected in love.

James 5:16 (ESV) – Therefore, confess your sins to one another and pray for one another, that you may be healed. The prayer of a righteous person has great power as it is working.

Hebrews 11:1 (ESV) – Now faith is the assurance of things hoped for, the conviction of things not seen.

1 Corinthians 15:33 (ESV) – Do not be deceived: 'Bad company ruins good morals.

John 1:14 (ESV) – And the Word became flesh and dwelt among us, and we have seen his glory, glory as of the only Son from the Father, full of grace and truth.

Luke 18:27 (ESV) – But he said, 'What is impossible with men is possible with God.'

Zephaniah 3:17 (ESV) – The Lord your God is in your midst, a mighty one who will save; he will rejoice over you with gladness; he will quiet you by his love; he will exult over you with loud singing. Therefore I have continued my faithfulness to you.

Jeremiah 29:11 (ESV) – For I know the plans I have for you, declares the Lord, plans for welfare and not for evil, to give you a future and a hope.

Ecclesiastes 9:10 (ESV) – Whatever your hand finds to do, do it with your might, for there is no work or thought or knowledge or wisdom in Sheol, to which you are going.

Psalm 46:10 (ESV) – Be still and know that I am God. I will be exalted among the nations; I will be exalted in the earth!

1 John 4:12 (ESV) – No one has ever seen God; if we love one another, God abides in us and his love is perfected in us.

1 John 3:1 (ESV) – See what kind of love the Father has given to us, that we should be called children of God; and so we are. The reason why the world does not know us is that it did not know him.

James 4: (ESV) – Submit yourselves therefore to God. Resist the devil, and he will flee from you.

James 1:2-4 (ESV) – Count it all joy, my brothers, when you meet trials of various kinds, for you know that the testing of your faith produces steadfastness. And let steadfastness have its full effect, that you may be perfect and complete, lacking in nothing.

Hebrews 11:6 (ESV) – And without faith it is impossible to please him, for whoever would draw near to God must believe that he exists and that he rewards those who seek him.

Hebrews 11:1-40 (ESV) – Now faith is the assurance of things hoped for, the conviction of things not seen.

Hebrews 4:16 (ESV) – Let us then with confidence draw near to the throne of grace, that we may receive mercy and find grace to help in time of need.

2 Timothy 1:7 (ESV) – For God gave us a spirit not of fear but of power and love and self-control.

Philippians 4:6 (ESV) – Do not be anxious about anything, but in everything by prayer and supplication with thanksgiving let your requests be made known to God.

Ephesians 2:10 (ESV) – For we are his workmanship, created in Christ Jesus for good works, which God prepared beforehand, that we should walk in them.

2 Corinthians 12:9 (ESV) – But he said to me, 'My grace is sufficient for you, for my power is made perfect in weakness.' Therefore I will boast all the more gladly of my weaknesses, so that the power of Christ may rest upon me.

2 Corinthians 5:17 (ESV) – Therefore, if anyone is in Christ, he is a new creation. The old has passed away; behold, the new has come.

## Some Final Thoughts

I would be remiss if didn't end this chapter with some notes as a Christian minister. While a lot has been said about being *unstoppable* and *relentless* in the secular sense, a lot can also be applied in the Christian life.

Can we be *relentless* and be Christian? I believe we can.

### Maxims I came up with based on the Word of God as well as quotes from others

1. The Lord God expects the best from us. This life is God's gift to us. What we do with it is *our* **gift to God**.
2. "Seek first the kingdom of God and all these things will be added to you." Matthew 6:33
3. You are blessed so that *you* can be a blessing to others.
4. Only one life will soon be past, only what's done for Christ will last.
5. Nothing happens unless you dream.
6. Do your best and God will take care of the rest.
7. "Die with memories not with dreams." ~Author Unknown
8. Blessed are those who dream and are willing to pay the price to make their dreams come true.
9. "This is the day which the Lord has made. Let us rejoice and be glad in it." Psalm 118:24. There is no other day like it. Use it. Be a blessing. Start your dream.

10. "The journey of a thousand miles begins with one step." ~Lao Tzu, Chinese philosopher
11. Do good. Do no harm. Always stay in love with God.

## More Questions to explore and ponder that will help you become a Relentless Leader

1. Do you know your leadership style?
2. Do you start with the end in mind? (based on Steven Covey's book "The 7 Habits of Highly Effective People)
3. Do I still have my life force? (based on

In conclusion, we've discussed the character traits of a *Relentless Leader*.

Start now. Don't be afraid to dream big. Have the courage to face life's challenges.

Reinvent yourself. Learn something new. Think outside the box. Create a new box.

It's never too late. Today is the first day of the rest of your life.

And remember…*the best is yet to come.*

*Standing L→R: Dante Jr., David and Stephen. Sitting L→R: Pastor Eleazar "Bong" and wife Vivelyn*

# REV. DANTE ELEAZAR "BONG" SIMON

 Dante Eleazar "Bong" Lorenzana Simon is an ordained United Methodist Pastor, having served for 35 years in local church communities in Metro Manila, Houston, Dallas, Los Angeles, and the San Francisco Bay areas.

In 2016, he reinvented himself and got trained as a professional Chaplain with the College of Pastoral Supervision and Psychotherapy at Kaiser Permanente.

Presently he is the Spiritual Care Director of Heartland Hospice, covering most of the San Francisco Bay area.

Bong had always wanted to write. With God's blessing and his friend and high school Classmate Jackie Morey's inspiration and help, this book is now his third Collaborative book.

Bong now thoroughly loves to write and continues to write. He also enjoys gardening, flower arranging, making bead bracelets, singing, and has composed a few songs himself.

Rev. Simon is blessed and happily married to Vivelyn Pascual and blessed with 3 wonderful sons David, Stephen and Dante Jr.

## CHAPTER 10
# Relentless Quest
By Paulyn Jean Rosell Ubial, M.D., M.P.H.

I have always thought that life is *not* about how far up you reach in the ladder of success or how much you have amassed of the treasures of this earth.

I've always felt that life is more about how many times you'd fallen and yet risen from struggles, trials, tribulations, and challenges. These make us better people and physicians, as we undertake the ultimate and most important measure of our lives: How many people we have touched and helped in life's journey.

In life, we take inspiration from others around us, and how they'd overcome the challenges and stumbles in life—how they'd risen back, to pick up the broken pieces of themselves and mended their lives back to a life of meaning and purpose...

Since my first days in the service of my fellowmen as a physician in a lonely town in far, far away **Mindanao** (the largest island in the Philippines) where I signed up at the

Department of Health (DOH) to be a Rural Health Practice Program (RHPP) Volunteer in October 1988, I had embraced this wonderful quotation attributed to Stephen de Grellet, a Quaker missionary during the time of the French Revolution.

> *"I shall pass this world but once. Any good or kindness I may show let me do it now for I may never pass this way again."*

I even stitched and framed this saying to be left behind in my Rural Health Unit. At that time, I was doing cross-stitch work as a hobby during my free time. Then I also cross-stitched this quotation into a pattern, and framed it for my City Health Office "family" where I later served as a remembrance gift. I think to this day it is displayed in the lobby of these health facilities.

When I graduated from the University of the East Ramon Magsaysay Memorial Medical Center (UERMMC) College of Medicine, and after the board exams and internship, it was tempting for me to take a traditional route of being a resident physician in a big modern hospital and become a "specialist", then a consultant, set up a clinic, and probably become a College of Medicine faculty member.

However, that was not what life had intended for me. For me at that point in my young career, the attraction of life was not about material gain or power or fame but it was about embracing change and opportunity, going on an adventure of self-discovery, finding out "my place in the sun,"…and being in the position where I could *help the most*.

We all look at life as either a "Glass half empty or half full." So much of life is about handling *challenges* and handling *perspective*.

**One powerful perspective is**: You could look at problems and challenges as opportunities for learning or growth!

I also did a cross stitch of the following favorite quote from "Desiderata" by Max Erhmann...

> *"Go placidly amid the noise and the haste and remember what piece there may be in silence as far as possible, without surrender, be good on good terms with all persons."*
>
> *"Speak your truth quietly and clearly and listen to others even the dull and ignorant they too have their story to tell."*

Well, it was there in an isolated, rural area of Mindanao where I spent my first few months as a physician, away from the comfort of family and friends, that I *realized* my real purpose in life.

I would pray and meditate a lot because there was really nothing else to do in my rented room in the house of our Rural Health Unit (RHU) Nurse, where she lived with her six young adult children. I would pray and let God lead me, and show me the way...

... my *realization* brought me through the years – all the way to the **highest position in government** for a medical doctor!

After 29 years of hard work, heartache and toil, my sincerity and dedication were recognized – and I was sworn in as the 28th Secretary of the Department of Health of the Philippines on June 30, 2016.

Never in my wildest dreams did I imagine that I would reach this point in my career – that of becoming the Secretary of Health. All I wanted to do when I graduated from Medical School was to "Help as many people as possible."

It sounds idealistic, but, truly, idealism brought me here.

Never be ashamed of verbalizing what is in your heart because that is the way we touch others and inspire them to join us in our quest for peace and purpose…and that quest may often lead us to the road less traveled.

After medical school I went to the University of the Philippines – Philippine General Hospital (UP PGH) as an intern, and there I realized I *couldn't* continue working in a hospital because there was *so* much misery and drudgery.

I went home every day with a heavy heart. And I couldn't stop crying whenever a patient would die.

There were even times when my fellow interns and I would shell out our own money to buy the medicines for them. We couldn't merely stand by and watch our patients suffer, when with the money in our pockets, we could buy the medicine that could heal them.

After one year of exhaustion and heartbreak, I told myself that there's got to be another field of medicine for me to embrace. My fellow doctors who persisted and endured the emotional stresses of hospital life, did what I *didn't* have the heart to do. But that was simply not the life for me.

## The Life of a Rural Doctor

Since my first day as a Rural Health Practice Program (RHPP) Volunteer in October 1988, my goal has always been to do my best and do what is right all the time, while trusting that God would lead me to the right path.

I had heard so many horror stories of how corrupt the people in government are, but I truly had *no* idea because I had never worked in government before nor had I ever experienced getting a job in the first place!

This RHPP Volunteer position was my first job and I was just excited to meet new people and do new things as a first time doctor, straight out of taking the medical board exams.

I was very excited to be on my own and to get my first salary or stipend (that's what they called our allowance, because technically we were not employed…we didn't have contracts).

I experienced so many new adventures at that time – like living on my own, away from my family for the first time, and working with the Rural Health Unit (RHU) staff, who were older than me…but who reported *to me* because I was the doctor.

However, experience-wise the staff probably knew more than I did. Here I was, with all my notes and books from

Medical School in tow. I met the Medical Health Officer (MHO), but she was seldom in the RHU, so I was basically in-charge.

My day started at 6am with breakfast. By 7am I was walking to the RHU which was just 10 minutes away from my boarding house.

I was there early, before the 8am opening time of the RHU; but many of the Barangay Health Workers (BHW) and some midwives would already be there in the RHU ahead of me ... talk about dedication!

They would clean the place before the doctor came in, so they were surprised to see me that early. They would tell me to come in at 8:30am or later so they could prepare the RHU and the patients. And yet I was excited to see the patients, so I was there early, every single day during my 6 months there as a Rural Practice Volunteer.

I would eagerly wait at the RHU hallway for the first patients to trickle in for the day. When I started out there were just a handful of patients. I wondered why people didn't come to the RHU.

I realized in the days to come that there were practices in the clinic the put patients off – it was *corruption* in its insidious form. Patients were asked to pay for Medicines that were supposed to be provided for free! Also, I discovered that previous doctors would come in late in the morning, and then leave for their private clinic practice just before lunchtime, and then never show up in the afternoon.

After this shocking discovery, I often asked myself: Was it only I who deemed this unacceptable? Or was I just overreacting about something totally the norm in these places?

Well, I did what I believed was right. I came in everyday at 7:30am and left the clinic at 5:30pm or until the last patient was seen and treated.

You see, I wanted to show everyone the way it ought to be in the RHU and not be swallowed up by the tide.

Our routine continued like this Mondays to Saturdays. We worked half days on Saturdays. It was rather busy on Saturdays because it was also market day in town. People came in for their check-up or health consultation, after which they would stop by the market.

It wasn't until my *second month* in the RHU that I realized that things were *not* as they seemed. Although we had a lot of patients, we *didn't* have enough supplies and medicines.

New supplies would *occasionally* come in, but oftentimes, I felt bad when I only had prescriptions to give to the poor patients – who really looked too poor to afford the medicines. Majority were farmers who didn't have much.

Most of my life I had lived in Manila where I saw poor, slum dwellers. And yet the poor in the rural areas seemed even *poorer* or shall I say "deprived".

It seemed they had very little access to health information and knowledge and tended to have much more traditional beliefs, health myths and misconceptions.

I'll never forget the 15-year old girl who came into my clinic with a baby in her arms. Looking at the baby girl, she seemed chubby and healthy, but on closer look, I diagnosed a malnutrition condition where the patient looked bloated and not emaciated! It was Kwashiorkor – a severe form of malnutrition!

I only saw descriptions of this condition in my books, *never* in the hospitals and clinics in Manila! I'd also seen this in my photos and videos of children in India and Pakistan.

Yet that day, I saw this condition right in front of me!

Candidly, I was quite excited to see a textbook case of Kwashiorkor with the cobble stone dermatitis and lethargic infant with generalized edema.

I asked the mother what she had been giving her baby. She replied, "Am" – which is the liquid that covers the rice before it comes to a boil when it's being cooked.

What?! I was shocked…and heartbreaking.

This was all the baby had been receiving, because the mother had no milk from her own breasts, and they didn't have money to buy formula. No wonder the baby was malnourished – all she had was water with some Vitamins from the rice wash… no calories, no minerals, no proteins!

No, I cannot forget these cases I saw in the boondocks of this sleepy town.

We would also go on medical missions to Bagobo Tribal villages. On one of these missions, I saw another textbook case of Bitot's spot (a cornea ulcer due to Vitamin A deficiency) of a young girl – who was described to be bumping objects and stumbling at night.

She had the classic "Night Blindness" that came with Vitamin A deficiency. I gave her our mega-dose of Vitamin A that UNICEF supplies to the RHU for free. In just one week after the mega-dose of Vitamin A, the ulcer on the cornea (surface of the eye) disappeared.

Similar to the baby with Kwashiorkor, I simply gave a mega-dose of Vitamin A and some advice to the mother to start re-lactation. After a week, I saw a more alert baby.

I consider the mega-dose of Vitamin A a real miracle drug – especially for the poor folks in rural areas with malnutritional disorders and deficiencies.

But to me, the real miracles were the end results in these patients' lives. Had I not been there to diagnose these conditions and giving the patients the wonder drug, what would have happened to them?

The baby might not have reached her first birthday because she could've succumbed to pneumonia or diarrhea. And the young girl with corneal ulcer would probably end up blind within a months' time, if I wasn't able to provide the wonder drug!

I felt the corruption and non-accountability of people in government in those areas had led to the sorry state of health of the country at that time.

You see, we had all the weapons, medicines and supplements to fight the common illnesses; but if doctors didn't show up and see these patients, how could we let the wonder drugs and pills to do their magic?

I truly pitied the poor in the hinterlands and rural settings. Indeed, they seemed poorer than their urban counterparts. They were passive zombies, just waiting for the scraps that government workers would dole out to them.

This was not like the poor in the Health Center in Manila; likely because of media exposure, they seemed more in-the-know and were rather demanding of the health care providers.

The rural poor had their hands and faces so dirty you'd think there was no water in their houses. They smelled of sweat and probably didn't bathe regularly. And they looked thin and hungry all the time!

This was why as much as possible I wanted to give them the medicines they needed because I knew for certain that, if I had merely given them *a prescription*, they likely couldn't buy what was written on it.

For children with pneumonia, we usually had Paracetamol Syrup and Amoxicillin Suspension and I would give them the full dose for 10 days that usually meant 4 bottles of 60ml suspension and 1 bottle paracetamol.

The "poor" mothers had difficulty carrying *all* the medicines we'd give them. But they were blessed because these medications were all complimentary, at *no* charge to them.

Then one day my MHO appeared. She saw what I was doing, called me aside to her office and told me, "*Doctora, don't give them all the medicines; we won't have enough for **other** patients. And you should charge them – even if only P5.00 per bottle so they will value it.*"

I was horrified that my MHO had even made these suggestions and comments! I knew that the medicines were supposed to be given *free* to the patients and that, if I only gave one or two bottles and the patient could not continue the full dose, this could result in anti-microbial resistance (AMR).

Anyway, after my MHO left, I still continued with what I was doing; I did not heed her advice whatsoever.

And because patients were likely happy and satisfied with what the nurses, midwives, BHWs, and I were doing, they gave *more* donations in the box labeled "Donations"!

It was an accepted practice at that time, but later on I would stop this practice in the DOH because occasionally, it was a source of corruption too. You see, during those days, donations were used to fund Christmas parties, raffles, and gifts to workers on special occasions.

But when I came to the RHU, since I would be there constantly, we had more and more patients, and we saw the increase in donations as well. From about 500 patients per month, we were collecting 3-4 thousand Pesos a month. That was a treasure back then, when my allowance from the DOH was only P1,600 a month.

We would put the money in the bank, and I together with the RHU staff would make plans on how we were to spend it wisely.

On my second month in the office, I had the whole RHU painted, then we bought small furniture such as chairs and benches. Later, we had curtains placed and we acquired my dream examination table, complete with pillow and blankets to cover the patient. We even purchased a sliding curtain barrier to give patients privacy.

I felt so fulfilled when I left the RHU because it was exceedingly better than when I first arrived.

Through the years, as I rose within the ranks of the DOH (Department of Health), I had first hand encounters with *corrupt practices.*

I believe that if one does nothing, then he/she is part of the problem. I would oftentimes write anonymous letters of complaint addressed directly to the Secretary of Health (SOH).

He/she would often send an investigation committee (a 2-3 person team) to the area, but they never interviewed me. Usually they talked to the MHO or head of the unit who would flippantly say that the complaint was "baseless" and that it was just some disgruntled employee who had made the complaint.

The SOH would then treat the team to a sumptuous dinner of the best seafoods and the glorious fruits of the area.

Everybody went home happy, the wrong practices stopped for a while, but these would then resume after 2-3 months.

I felt so frustrated at that time; I seriously thought of leaving the DOH.

But the thought that entered my mind was that if I left, what would happen then? It would be like giving up because the situation seemed hopeless – when I believed that there was *no such thing* as a hopeless situation.

I believe that we need to keep hammering at the system until it changes and is molded to the way we want, a **corruption-free one**!

There were times when UNICEF, WHO or USAID provided us money to undertake trainings of health workers. I was very frugal on those occasions thinking the more money we saved, the more trainings and activities we could do.

However, it completely shocked me when I submitted my first "utilization report" on the money spent for training "Hilots" (Traditional Birth Attendants [TBAs] ).

Here's what happened. Instead of spending Php800 per person per day, I was able to do it at 350 per person per day…and returned more than half the allotted funds. The DOH Manager was apparently shocked and told me, *"Doctora, don't do this…you have to redo your Utilization Report to reflect that you spent **all** the money on the training needs of the participants! If you submit this report, the other Local Governments will get pissed **at you**… because you will prove that the trainings* *can be done on a cheaper budget, so UNICEF will bring down the allotment!"*

Oh my, they wanted me to lie! What had been happening was that huge amounts of money would continue to be given by UNICEF, and the managers would end up dividing the amount amongst the participant to "take home"!

It would've been good if they did this all the time – so that a lot of "poorly-paid" public health workers have a share in the Foreign assistance. But I also heard that in many instances, the Trainers completely pocketed the extra amount and would ask their friend-establishments to provide the Official Receipts (OR) as proofs of disbursement.

Sadly, *this* was the norm in the DOH…until a few of us "young" doctors arrived, newly-hired at the DOH – who told the older staff that this was not right and should be stopped.

Well, we triumphed because we ended this "accepted" corrupt practice right there. Some people in the DOH and the LGU (Local Government Unit) partners hated us for that, but we conveyed that it was the right thing to do.

We returned unused funds and reprogrammed it for other worthwhile and meaningful health activities and bought other important commodities.

When it comes to corruption, sometime people just accept it as the norm, because everyone benefits from it. But what people rarely realize is that if you *do not* spend the budget or allocation properly, you are actually depriving other sectors and individuals the access to important commodities and services.

## Rising through the Ranks in the Bureaucracy

As I rose through the ranks, I heard *many* stories about corrupt practices, but I did not have first-hand experience of these practices such as: the sale of the milk powder donations of USAID to the local ice cream factory, the sale of the Burgur and Green peas donations from UNICEF to hog raisers, ghost deliveries of drugs and medicines, pocketing of UNICEF and WHO funds for training activities with signatures of " ghost participants " as proof of use of the funds, and payment of half the quoted price for the venue and hotel in connivance with their representatives, *"padulas"* (a bribe), *"pasalubong"* (a gift for loved ones when they return from travels), etc.

In my entire 29 years with DOH, I was never involved in these activities. I often asked the staff why this was so, and they would tell me that the suppliers were saying, "We would never attempt to bribe Dra. Ubial because 'malayo pa lang nakabusina na!'" (She would blow her horn and tell on us, even from far away!)

I always felt that it was a good turn of events because I didn't know whether, if faced with the temptation, I could actually resist it.

When it came to situations actually encountered by my other colleagues, I would tell them to file a complaint or affidavit and that I would personally support them.

Some did file, others were afraid…and still others thought it was useless to do so.

There was one time our Licensing Officer was *known* to be extorting money from the hospitals that he would inspect.

I told his Division Chief about this, *"I don't have direct information and knowledge of this activity, but you do, and if you file a case against him with CSC or OMB, I will support you."*

But astonishingly, the Division Chief merely said, *"Ma'am, kawawa naman (pity him). He has 8 children and if he loses his job what would happen to the children. I propose we just move him to have no direct contact with the clients and the hospitals."* So we did. We moved him to backdoor operations of the Division and I told my Division Chief to put everything in writing because I firmly believe that "If it was not written, it did not happen!"

I discovered through the years working in government that *fighting corruption* is a **never ending endeavor**. One must be **relentless**, never waiver in one's commitment and seriousness to make a difference, and take steps to change the "accepted" or status quo of the systems and operations.

I felt that if I were to go up higher in the ladder of hierarchy of the DOH, I could do even more, and effect better changes to curb corruption.

When I was promoted to Assistant Secretary in April 2008, I told myself that, as a member of the highest policy making body of the DOH, I could effect changes that would be sustainable and *forever* impact the way we did things at the DOH.

In 2009, I became head of the Integrity Development Committee (IDC) and effected the many changes I had dreamed of since I joined DOH as a rural practice volunteer in Kidapawan North Cotabato in 1988!

We produced the **Code of Conduct and Ethical Behavior** for the DOH.

Can you believe it? This was the first time we came out with specific guidelines for DOH and the health sector. We usually previously just relied on the Civil Service Commission (CSC) guidelines and Republic Act (RA) 6713.

Due to this new document, I was probably able to forever change the way we did things at the DOH, especially by coming out with a "NO GIFTS POLICY" and putting up these signages throughout the DOH offices and the hospitals.

This practice was also adopted eventually in other government agencies such as the Civil Aviation Authority of the Philippines, the Department of Social Welfare and Development, the Department of Education, etc.

Because of our work in the Integrity Development Committee, I would also find myself faced with several court cases, ombudsman, and civil service cases filed *against* me.

It seems that fighting corruption often also involves fighting cases filed against the crusaders themselves. In fact, those who engage in corrupt practices seem to be in better positions because they have the money, the connections and the resources to harass the crusaders. If it were not for the camaraderie we had in the IDC, we would have been demoralized and would've easily given up the fight.

There was one particular DOH Regional Director whose list of corrupt acts could fill an entire book!

She purchased overpriced medicines, and did supplier-driven procurements. For example, malaria drugs for 200,000 patients were procured, when the actual number of malaria cases in the region was only 26 in any given year!

She also used office resources for unofficial transactions (such as charging the DOH for her personal long distance telephone calls and for courier services to transport her furniture and dogs home to her home province), etc.

She was found guilty in one of the cases filed against her and, although she had already retired when the decision was handed down, her punishment included depriving her of her GSIS pension (the Government Service Insurance System in the Philippines).

The above-mentioned Regional Director filed harassment cases against me and two other members of the IDC. And for the next ten years she filed other cases against us in various venues (the Office of the Ombudsman, the Civil Service Commission, the Office of the President, and the Professional Regulatory Commission).

Thankfully, these cases were *all* dismissed. But unfortunately we, the innocent parties, had to pay our lawyer's fees out of our own pockets, and had to use our valuable time and energy to attend the hearings and prepare all affidavits, counter-affidavits and pleadings.

One case, a civil case in the Regional Trial Court that she had filed in her home town in Region II in June 2009, was finally resolved in our favor in December 2019.

I've noticed that the people who engage in corrupt practices are the people who are bold and relentless in fighting the crusaders against corruption. If these persons exist at the DOH, it is probable that they can be found in the whole of government.

Oftentimes I think back and ask myself if fighting corruption was worth all the trouble. I'd spent a lot of resources, energy and sleepless nights to address the persistent harassment.

Was it really worth it? I could've had an easier time in the DOH by simply turning a blind eye towards corruption. I could have just concentrated on doing my job without getting involved in the fight against corruption at the DOH.

Through the years, I moved further up the ladder of the government hierarchy and became the Secretary of Health in July 2016. I unexpectedly realized that being labelled a corruption crusader was in fact a disadvantage!

People were afraid of me and what I could do, including the members of Congress which became evident during my Commission on Appointments (CA) hearing.

They would throw corruption and incompetence allegations

against me without any basis or proof, and merely based on statements of individuals who opposed my being the Secretary of Health.

I was deeply saddened to have been rejected by the Commission on Appointments because it just showed that persons who made false accusations against an anti-graft crusaders like me, could win the hearts and minds of legislators.

Was it really *that* easy to get rid of an anti-graft crusader? What did I do wrong? Was relying on my track record and background of integrity not enough to win an appointment?

That day, I felt that not only did I lose but the **entire bureaucracy** and **our country** also lost in our unending, **relentless** quest for a better and corrupt-free government.

## Life After Government Service

Thirty-three years have passed since my graduation as a member of the UERM Medicine Batch 1987. I spent the last 33 years as an Intern at UP PGH for one year, as a Rural Practice Volunteer in a faraway town in Mindanao for six months, in between jobs for three months, wondering what to do after passing the Medicine Board Exams in February-March 1989, followed my heart, joined the DOH Region 12 Office, and the rest is history.

I was at the DOH for 29 years. My illustrious career as a Public Service officer was abruptly terminated when the

Commission on Appointments passed a rejection verdict on my Ad Interim appointment as Secretary of Health.

Now two years and five months after that fateful day, I can actually say that I am very fortunate! The Lord spared me from being in the top leadership position of the DOH during its most difficult times.

The Dengvaxia fiasco came out mere months *after* my rejection in December 2017.

Then there was the measles outbreak in 2018 followed by various health emergencies in 2019.

There were continued measles epidemics throughout the country not just in the National Capital Region (NCR), then the diphtheria outbreak, the dengue outbreak, and the polio outbreak in July 2019.

In October 2019, there was the earthquake in Mindanao...

...and then the Taal Volcano eruption in January 2020.

As of this writing – the Corona Virus-19 disease pandemic began in March 2020.

I had thought that the worst health emergency *ever* was typhoon (hurricane) Yolanda, which hit the Visayas Region in November 2013 when I was the Assistant Secretary of Health for the Visayas!

During the 3rd year Anniversary commemoration of typhoon Yolanda on Nov. 8, 2016, I was with Philippine President Rodrigo Duterte's party that went to Tacloban City to join the commemoration activities. I thought to myself – seeing the resiliency of the "Warays" (people who speak the Waray dialect) in Tacloban, Leyte and Samar provinces – after they rose above the destruction of Hurricane Yolanda, we could indeed rise against *any* challenge…as a Nation!

When the Marawi Siege happened in May 2017, I was with the President in Camp Evangelista in Cagayan de Oro City during which he pinned medals gave cellphones, a new hand gun, a check and cash gifts to 63 wounded soldiers from Marawi.

I was teary eyed when the President pointed to me saying, "Ilongga iyang si Dra, matapang yan! Isog na!" (That Dr. Ubial who's an Ilongga [a lady from the Iloilo province] is courageous! Very brave!)

It was at that moment that I became more resolute to work for peace in Mindanao, for the health of the Filipinos, and for the development and prosperity of my beloved Philippines!

I love this country and I am glad to have been able to serve it with a President who resolved to bring out the best in all of us in the Executive Branch, and to rally the entire nation into a vision of hope and prosperity for all Filipinos: "Ambisyon Natin 2040, Maginhawang Buhay Para Sa Lahat ng Pilipino", translated, "Our Ambition 2040: A Comfortable Life for All Filipinos."

I am honored and pleased to have worked with a President who abhors corruption and illegal drugs, who has compassion for the poor and marginalized, and who cares for the soldiers, teachers and other government employees of this country. Exceptionally honored!

Little did I know back then, that in a few short months I would no longer be part of the government.

My rejection on October 10, 2017 did not come as a shock. I was actually preparing for it months in advance.

In September 2017, after Congressman Harry Roque congratulated me for my appointment as Secretary of Health, he recommended someone I knew to be very corrupt as head of the Philippine Health Insurance Corporation (PhilHealth).

During the Commission on Appointment hearing, when Cong. Roque made a power point presentation with allegations of how "corrupt" I was, I challenged him to file cases against me with the Ombudsman or with the Office of the President.

Then there were more in opposition to me, including PhilHealth Member of the Board, and my predecessor, the former Secretary of Health.

I knew then that my fate was sealed. These were politically entrenched people, and I had no political backing whatsoever. In fact some members of Congress who sat at the CA called me the day before the final CA hearing and told me that I should go talk to some members of Congress – those very ones who had the power with just a phone call to ask the CA to reject me.

The other members of Congress who believed in me said that they couldn't go against the wishes of the more powerful ones because they wouldn't get their projects funded nor assigned to Committee positions.

It was evident that politics was more important than 29 years of my clean record and honest and excellent performance.

So, I was rejected.

I was the *fifth* Cabinet appointee of President Duterte to be rejected by this CA whose members professed that they were one with the President in his call to ensure that CHANGE IS COMING! Yet it seemed that for the CA, change had not come.

It turned out to be a matter of mere political exercise, wherein it wasn't important to them that I had a corrupt-free track record and proven history of dedicated services that resulted in outstanding performance.

Perhaps this may sound like sour grapes to some…maybe, but the truth has to be told.

Now, as I write this – two years and five months out of government service, my pace of living has slowed down quite a lot.

During my entire career at the DOH, I never received "envelopes" – which signify bribes.

I would often innocently and in jest ask, "*Saan naman yang mga envelope na iyan; bakit walang nakakarating sa akin?*" [English:

Where did all those "envelopes" go? Why hasn't any reached me?]

I recall my staff in the Davao Region would tell me, *"Kasi Ma'am sabi nila, malayo pa lang nakabusina na kayo, kaya they do not even attempt, baka sampalin nyo sila ng pera!"* [English: You see, Ma'am, they say that should they even attempt to get an "envelope" to you, while the envelope is still afar and on it's way to you, you'd already call them out. They say you might even slap them with the money inside!]

I wonder to this day – if someone had attempted to give me an envelope with money back then, would I have had the strength of character or the will power to refuse? Well, it never happened, so I'm very glad about this!

But these days, I do get envelopes and yes, I do accept them!

I speak at conferences and the organizers give me an envelope containing an honorarium between P2,000 to as much as P10,000.

There was one corporate event by a private company that had a Strategic Planning Workshop, wherein I gave a two-hour lecture on the Philippine Health Situation. I received the biggest lecturer's fee ever – PhP30,000! I'd never received such as huge amount in my entire career at DOH!

I would have had to work *10 days* just to get *that* amount with my salary at the DOH – *not two hours*! My goodness, how much does the private sector pay their doctor-managers? I wonder…

Now that I am no longer in Government service, and instead, I work with NGOs (Non-Governmental Organizations), I realize that the compensation still doesn't matter much. I get enough finances, even though it may not be as regular as every 15$^{th}$ and 30th of the month, which is the case in government service.

At this point in my life, things have slowed down, but I believe I'm still helping other people, though on a smaller scale – and I'm still finding fulfilment as a healer and leader.

I continue my advocacies to fight corruption, help the poor and the marginalized, and to do the right thing all the time.

Which part of the health sector you are from, is not important. What is important is to keep fighting, keep contributing, and to never never give up.

I always tell people *"Habang may buhay, may pag-asa"* (While there is life, there is hope). And my favorite motto from the words of slain U.P. activist Lean Alejandro, *"Kung hindi ako, sino? Kung hindi ngayon, kailan?"* (If not me, then who? If not now, then when?).

## What Next?

"I shall not pass through this world again; any good or kindness I may do let me do it now, for I may never pass this way again."

Remember this is my favorite quotation from Stephen de Grellet? It delights my heart to know that the cross stitch pattern I made of this quote still hangs to this day at the City

Health Office of Cotabato City – where I served for two years during the early part of my career in the DOH.

I can't help but think about the many employees back then, who were already callous to corruption, and considered the poor patients as burdens instead of opportunities to serve God!

It has been very different from how I viewed my vocation as a doctor. To me, it's not about the pay or the work to be accomplished, it is all about serving God by serving others… the pay was just incidental.

Again, let me end my piece by stating this…

Life is not about how much wealth or success we have amassed or attained. It is about how many people we have touched and how we have made this world a better place than when we found it.

I still believe that the fight for a better world, a less corrupt world, must be a **relentless** one. There must be no let up.

Then perhaps we could have something to say to the Creator when we finally meet Him at the end of our life's journey.

We must never stop trying. Be **relentless** in accomplishing our goals and making this world a better place. By God's grace we move forward and continue the fight.

> "Life is not about how much wealth or success we have amassed or attained. It is about how many people we have touched and how we have made this world a better place than when we found it."
>
> ~Paulyn Rosell Ubial, M.D., M.P.H.

I also know several honest and sincere public servants who had cases filed *against* them. They left Government *without* benefits and instead, with a penalty of dismissal from the service – when they had **not** done anything illegal or immoral!

It really seems unfair because these people did not directly participate in the corrupt practices, and yet they were the ones punished.

I can attest to the fact that government work is a thankless job.

Nobody recognizes your hard work, nor the daily grind in your small corner of the bureaucracy. If indeed one is recognized, many of these would be the flamboyant personalities who were only seeking attention when they entered public service. And likely their end goal was to seek a high position or an elective office in the government.

Such was not my goal. Never did I dream of becoming an elected government official let alone a Cabinet Member.

My experience as the Secretary of Health (SOH) was *not* a bed of roses; it was difficult especially because I did not and still do not belong to any political party.

I don't speak in political jargon. I did not understand the unspoken messages when politicians would call me to their offices asking for projects, they would telephone governors, mayors and other political allies, and then tell me to talk to them about the promised projects in their areas.

I would often tell the politician, *"I have no qualms or hesitation with providing projects in your areas of jurisdiction, since all these inputs will benefit the people whom we vowed to serve and whose taxes are paying for the projects."* But I would say further, *"Since these funds go to the people, Sir/Madam, and **not** to your pockets, I have no problem with projects for your area at all!!!"*

And the rest is history.

I rose through the ranks in the health sector of the country.

After my stint as a Rural Health Primary Physician, I joined the Region XII Health Office in Cotabato as a Medical Specialist I, and was in-charge of the Maternal and Child Health Program as well as the Breastfeeding Program.

After only a few months in the Regional Health Office XII, I became an Assistant City Health Officer (ACHO) in Cotabato City under Mayor Vic Badoy, the nation's youngest mayor at that time.

According to the DOH Human Resources (HR) people processing my appointment, the mayor had said, *"She is actually not qualified. But because there are no other takers who are qualified* (one needs 5 years' experience), *she can be appointed to that position."*

DOH HR also informed me that it was very unusual for a new graduate to get such a high position in government!

After two years in Cotabato City, I applied for the DOH Central Office Polio Eradication program. Thus, I moved back to Manila.

I also headed other programs and projects of the DOH in my 29-year career such as "Sentrong Sigla" – the Quality Assurance program of the DOH, and the "Red Orchid Awards" – the Tobacco Control advocacy program in the DOH.

Lo and behold, after 29 years of sincere public service, I became the *only* Secretary of Health to have come from the grassroots!

I worked in cities and provinces all over the Philippines: Kidapawan, Cotabato, Manila, Iloilo, Zamboanga, Davao, Manila, Leyte during the Yolanda response and rehabilitation operations, then back Manila.

After 29 years in the DOH, I was appointed as the 28th Health Secretary of the nation.

What is my advice to Public Relations (PR) people?

Don't aim for a higher position for the purpose of an exalted status. Instead, just do your best in any endeavor, and let God take care of the rest.

For all my 29 years in the DOH, I can proudly say that I am one doctor who never received a professional fee (PF) for my services! I treated hundreds even thousands of patients but I never asked for a PF. I may not be rich in wealth, but I am rich in happiness and fulfillment.

I know and can confidently say that I have served my God, my country, and my fellowman to the best of my ability. And I can also proudly say, "There is no shame in my career – there is no shame to what I have gone through in my life."

There is no shame that I was *not* confirmed by the Commission on Appointments because I refused to dance to the tune of the traditional politicians of the House of Representatives or the Senate…and I am proud of this.

I am also proud to say that I experienced everything that I had gone through in the government because I was never a yes-ma'am or yes-sir type of health leader. And I knew when it was the right time to stand firm on my beliefs.

I had once said in a congressional inquiry that *"Health and politics should never mix."*

Let me elaborate on this statement. I believe that *"There should be no politics and ideology in the health sector, and in both services and priorities, our decisions must always be based on science."*

## To our youth

The future is in front of you and nobody can tell who among you could be a future Health Secretary, the first head of Centers for Disease Control of the Philippines, or maybe even the first head of a modern vaccine production facility in our country.

That's what I'm focusing on at present. I am working with Senator Richard Gordon on the pertinent bills because I know that these bills will help pave the way for the future of the Philippine healthcare system.

So much has changed in the health system since I myself graduated from UERMMC College of Medicine 33 years ago. The People Power Revolution (also known as the EDSA Revolution) – occurred in 1986 when I was in my 3rd year of Medical School.

There was much uncertainty as to whether or not I would even graduate.

At that time, I, together with my six other siblings, took to the streets and found myself *facing tanks* at EDSA – the main highway where hundreds of thousands of Filipinos demonstrated.

Then after I graduated, I volunteered for a six-month rural practice in Mindanao - in Kidapawan, North Cotabato. I became the *youngest* Assistant City Health Officer in the country in 1990 at 27 years old.

In 1991, health services were devolved to the local governments due to the Local Government Act, and then in 1995, the PhilHealth law was passed.

Aside from these two laws, and throughout my career at the DOH, there were various laws that had been passed which *changed the landscape* of the Philippine health care system: i) the Clean Air Act of 2000; ii) the Tobacco Control Act of 2004; iii) the Reproductive Health Law of 2013; iv) the Mental Health Law; and v) the Universal Health Law of 2018!

All these milestone laws and upheavals in the health system have forever changed how we deliver health services in this country – for better or for worse.

And in my own little way, I have helped, both in the background and in the foreground, by becoming part of this positive change.

I did it because of a calling. Passivity was never in my blood, and the call to service always whispered to me, like a tiny voice in my head.

## To my fellow Medical Doctors

To my fellow doctors – the state of passivity and of merely sitting back is dishonorable for us, because as physicians, we are *always* social movers – *never* bystanders.

In 1991, Pinatubo erupted, and at the time, we thought that the world had changed forever. We were exposed to the reality of the global climate changing and getting back at us.

Throughout the years, so many strong typhoons hit the country, thus creating more great challenges to our health system. We were ravaged by typhoons (hurricanes) Reming, Ondoy, Sendong, Pablo, and Yolanda, to name a few.

I was among the first responders of the DOH in Tacloban City, four days after it had been hit by Yolanda. I wept upon seeing the devastation she had wrought as I flew into Leyte from Cebu in a helicopter - my first chopper ride ever.

So many firsts happened to me during the Yolanda rehabilitation and recovery. We had no food, no water, no fuel, and meager resources. All 300 patients and 200 staff of Eastern Visayas Regional Medical Center were all looking to me for answers. I was the highest ranking DOH official then, at our devastated end referral hospital!

Shifting our focus to present day – we face another upheaval of the health care system. The SARS-COV-2 coronavirus causing the COVID-19 disease led to the first large-scale, global pandemic since the Spanish Flu pandemic of 1917.

It has changed and is changing our health care practices, our economy, and our very lives! We are facing insurmountable odds in the health system, and during this pandemic, life will become worse before it gets better.

Again, life is not about how far up you reach in the ladder of success or how much you have amassed of the treasures on this earth. Life is and has always been about the times you had fallen down and risen from all the struggles, trials, tribulations, and challenges.

The many times we've gone against the tide of *insurmountable odds* define who we are as a person. Will *you* challenge the status quo, or be carried by the tide and just take the easy way out?

At present, I am a volunteer at Quezon Institute's Mild COVID-19 Isolation Facility (MCIF) as the Facility Manager, and at the Philippine Red Cross (PRC) as the Head of the Molecular Laboratories during these trying times.

Why did I do so? I could have simply stayed at home. I wouldn't go hungry.

Yet I know who I am – a Health Worker, and a Medical Doctor. So I stepped up to the plate, ready to join the battle against COVID-19 because my calling is to be on the front lines!

I am ready to serve today and always.

Let us all be ready to face life's challenges and to not turn our backs on our committed profession. We must be **relentless** in our quest for a better Philippines and a better world!

L →R: Son Karl, Dr. Paulyn, Husband Edwin

# Paulyn Jean Rosell Ubial, M.D., M.P.H.

Paulyn Jean Rosell Ubial also fondly known as Doc Paulyn has 29 years of experience in Public Health. She graduated with a B.S. Zoology degree from the University of the Philippines (U.P.) Diliman, Quezon City, Doctor of Medicine from University of the East Ramon Magsaysay Memorial Medical Center (UERMMMC), did her Post-Graduate Internship at U.P. Philippine General Hospital and earned her Masters in Public Health from the University of the Philippines, Manila.

Starting as a Rural Health Practice Volunteer in Kidapawan, North Cotabato in 1988, she rose through the ranks to the highest government position at the Department of Health (DOH) in the Philippines – as Secretary of Health.

Dr. Ubial has received the Ten Outstanding Young Women of Cotabato City Award, became one of the youngest Assistant City Health Officers, was nominated as Outstanding Career Executive Service Officer, and received the Haydee Yorac Leadership Award.

Her Expertise is in Women's Health, Maternal, Neonatal and Child Health Programs.

She held top positions in other DOH Programs and Projects such as: Head of the Polio Eradication Unit, Founding Program Manager of Women's Health and Development, the Steering Committee Chair of the Red Orchid Awards (the Search for 100% Tobacco-Free Environment for LGUs, Government Offices & Government Hospitals), Head of Task Force for Performance Governance System and Social Dialogue, and Vice Chair of the Integrity Management Committee.

At present, Dr. Ubial is an Adjunct Professor at the University of the Philippines (U.P.) College of Public Health, she's a Red Cross Volunteer, President of Rise Against Hunger, Physicians for Peace MOB, and a Consultant for various Health Projects.

# PLEASE RATE OUR BOOK

My Collaborative-Authors and I would be honored if you would please take a few moments to rate our book on Amazon.com (U.S.).

Or, if you're in any of these countries, please use these Amazon sites:

    Amazon.ca (Canada)    Amazon.de (Germany)
    Amazon.co.uk (U.K.)    Amazon.co.jp (Japan)
    Amazon.com.au (Australia)    Amazon.com.mx (Mexico)
                                Amazon.es (Spain)
    Amazon.fr (France)

A 5-star rating *and* a short review (e.g. "Jam-packed with lessons on being RELENTLESS!" or "Thoroughly enjoyed it!") would be much appreciated. We welcome longer, positive comments as well.

If you feel like this book should be rated at three stars or fewer, please hold off posting your comments on Amazon. Instead, please send your feedback directly to me (Jackie), so that we can use it to improve the next edition. We're committed to providing the best value to our customers and readers, and your thoughts can make that possible.

You can reach me at CustomerStrategyAcademy@gmail.com.

Thank you very much!

To your success and prosperity with a purpose,

*Jackie Morey*

Publisher-Collaborative Author
CustomerStrategyAcademy@gmail.com

Manufactured by Amazon.ca
Bolton, ON